D0641040

THE BIOSYNTHESIS OF NATURAL PRODUCTS

THE BIOSYNTHESIS OF NATURAL PRODUCTS

An Introduction to Secondary Metabolism

JOHN D. BU'LOCK, PhD

Department of Chemistry, The University of Manchester

McGRAW-HILL PUBLISHING COMPANY LIMITED
LONDON
NEW YORK   TORONTO   SYDNEY

Published by
McGraw-Hill Publishing Company Limited
McGraw-Hill House, Maidenhead, Berkshire, England

94015

THIS BOOK HAS BEEN SET, PRINTED AND BOUND IN GREAT BRITAIN BY
SPOTTISWOODE, BALLANTYNE AND COMPANY LIMITED, LONDON AND COLCHESTER

Foreword

Biochemistry is concerned with the details of the transformations and interactions of biological molecules at all levels of organization. Ultimately it may be possible to explain many of the processes in terms recognizable to the classical chemist, although the enormous complexity of structure encountered may defeat a total explanation in these terms. In the meantime, it is very interesting and instructive to look at a field where the chemist and biochemist are already quite happy. The processes of biosynthesis of relatively simple molecules have reached a considerable degree of definition through their combined work. The chemist has often been able to predict overall schemes of biosynthesis on the basis of a knowledge of the availabilities and reactivities of building units. The biochemist has frequently been able to confirm these schemes, with much added detail, and to discover unpredicted schemes of his own. These provide the chemist with the further congenial task of explaining them in mechanistic terms.

On the experimental side great advances have recently been made with isotopic tracer techniques, the use of mutants and the isolation of enzymes.

The subject is one of the most active and intellectually satisfying on the border between the biological and physical sciences. To deal adequately with it requires either a team of experts, when the result is liable to be uneven in treatment and patchy in coverage, or else an unusual author who has a profound knowledge of chemistry and biochemistry, and is at least a practical biologist. Such a man is Dr J. D. Bu'Lock. He began his scientific life as a chemist, and carried out good original work in organic chemistry. The topics in which he was interested led him, first, into more chemical fields of biochemistry and, finally, into biological aspects of the development of microorganisms. He still spans the whole spectrum in interest and in experimental work.

The present book gives not only an up-to-date account of the facts, but presents points of view which the chemist, the biochemist and the biologist will all recognize as valid. A valuable feature is the inclusion of sections dealing with the experimental side of the subject.

Department of Biological   A. J. BIRCH
    and Organic Chemistry,
University of Manchester

Preface

The varied character of natural products, and indeed their very existence, pose many fundamental questions to botanists and micro-biologists; their industrial exploitation is already of considerable importance; their chemistry seems to offer endless possibilities. Every aspect of natural product study raises the question of the origins of these fascinating substances. In this book I have tried to outline the present knowledge of their origin, to show how that knowledge has been attained (largely through the work of organic chemists), and to show how this information can contribute to a deeper understanding of living organisms. In seeking to introduce the topic to those unfamiliar with it, whether chemists or biologists by training, I have not attempted an exhaustive compilation, but have preferred to illustrate the underlying general principles in this seemingly divided subject. Ten years ago, a comparable study would have been mainly a collection of hypotheses; let the present account be taken as a small tribute to those who have given the subject its experimental foundation.

JOHN D. BU'LOCK

Contents

CHAPTER ONE

Introductory

Primary and Secondary Metabolites

This book attempts to outline the origins of a great variety of compounds such as alkaloids, antibiotics, terpenes and so on, which have for many years been the peculiar interest of organic chemists but which, despite their natural origin, remain unfamiliar to most biochemists. The names of the natural products which enliven chemical indices, from abietic acid and ajmaline to zierone and zingiberene, do not adorn *J. Biol. Chem.*; conversely, few natural product chemists could distinguish between UDPG and dApT. The truth is that in "natural product chemistry" and in biochemistry we normally deal with two quite different selections of biological molecules, and only quite recently have the two disciplines found the common ground to which this book is devoted.

Occasionally, it is true, biochemistry of the classical kind has turned up problems that would interest and challenge the organic chemist, like the structures of the B-vitamins or the stereochemistry of DPNH, but most of the chemists' problems have been posed by substances of a different kind. Operationally, indeed, we could easily distinguish between "chemists' compounds" and "biochemists' compounds", but since we are here concerned to break down such conceptual barriers, it is fortunate that equivalent but less tendentious labels also exist.

The distinction between *primary* and *secondary* metabolites appears to have been first drawn by plant physiologists, who thus characterized, on the one hand, the substances which could be detected in practically all plants, and which seemed to be functional constituents such as chlorophyll or the lipids, and, on the other, a variety of substances each of which could be obtained only from particular plant species, and which accordingly could be assigned no general function (e.g. camphor or the tannins). Today, such a distinction is generally recognized and its application is no longer restricted to higher plants. It is accepted that there are basic patterns of primary metabolism on which the variety of organic systems imposes relatively minor modifications, and we can define secondary metabolites as having a restricted taxonomic distribution, as being products which are not formed under all circumstances, and as having no obvious metabolic function. The category is mainly defined in terms of chemical structure but in practical terms it also includes cases where a normal primary metabolite is produced in a disproportionate amount. The "biochemists' compounds" are, then, the primary metabolites, occurring in virtually the same pattern from microbes to mammoths, which express the fundamental unity of living matter; the "chemists' compounds", the "natural products" of our title, are the secondary metabolites, bizarre compounds from restricted sources, which express the individuality of species in chemical terms. Most correctly, the biochemists have directed their main attention to the primary metabolic processes, and today these are largely elucidated.

Meanwhile pharmacognosy, chemotherapy and, above all, the curiosity of chemists, enormously extended our knowledge of the range of secondary metabolites, whose variety seems inexhaustible. The determination of their chemical structures has been an enormous task—though now greatly simplified by modern investigative methods —but this provided only the raw materials for a true understanding of the natural products. So long as each new structure remained an individual curiosity, representing merely a single product from a single source, the natural products remained biochemically meaningless. However, chemists are accustomed to the challenge of synthesis as well as of analysis, and are accustomed to viewing molecular structures as summaries of the synthetic processes by which they might arise. Viewing the natural products in this way they soon found that a degree of order could be detected if their variety was interpreted in biogenetic terms. Painstakingly, and not without false starts, the structures were anatomized and compared; in particular, the terpenes and the alkaloids were slowly brought into order. By about 1950, the main biogenetic categories could be outlined much as we see them today, but still only in terms of hypothetical transformations, which convinced chemists wholly, and biologists not at all. In particular, the crucial linkages between primary and secondary metabolism remained inaccessible; the compounds which are simultaneously intermediates in the primary network and precursors for the radiating secondary pathways remained unidentified. The reacting entities could be referred to only in guarded terms—formaldehyde-or-its-equivalent, phenyl-alanine-or-a-closely-related-compound, and so on.

Even today, for reasons which we do not fully understand, the actual machinery of secondary biosynthesis remains surprisingly inaccessible (but *see* Chapter Five). However, the introduction of isotopic labelling methods, in the 1950s, offered a tool with which secondary biosynthesis could be studied experimentally in intact biological systems, and thus provided the subject with an observational basis. Though they are by no means the only source of data, such methods are undoubtedly the most widely applied in this field, and it has seemed useful to include sections dealing with their scope and limitations in the present account (Chapters Three and Nine). Most of the data for this book, in fact, come from experiments of this kind. In selecting subject-matter I have tried, so far as possible, to consider only those topics for which reasonable experimental data are available, and to avoid those exercises in paper-chemistry which chemists alone enjoy. It is, therefore, all the more satisfactory to note that the main outlines which thus emerge coincide broadly with those constructed *ex hypothesi* in the intuitive understanding of the pioneers. If the restriction has meant that some favoured topics have been excluded, let that be taken as a challenge to experimentalists!

The Precursors

The first and most significant results from the experimental investigation of secondary metabolism has been the identification of those foci in the primary network from which the secondary pathways derive. Structural anatomization alone was sufficient to collect the natural products into successively wider and wider groupings, defined in biogenetic terms, such as the four major categories forming our principal chapters here. To have brought together into intelligible relationships such diverse substances as squalene and gibberellic acid, or oleic acid and oxytetracycline, is itself a major scientific achievement. However, these biogenetic categories are ultimately defined in terms of common precursors which, once identified, constitute the linkages with primary metabolism. One of the remarkable and significant features of secondary metabolism which then emerges is, that it utilizes a very limited selection of such precursors, and that these precursors are also substances of special importance in primary metabolism. Figure 1.1 attempts to illustrate this in terms of the main pathways of carbon metabolism; such a presentation is instructive, though unfortunately it does not lend itself to a similar demonstration of other important connections, notably those which involve oxidation-reduction reactions (hydrogen metabolism) and "energy-rich" substrates (phosphate metabolism). In fact, both primary and secondary metabolic processes of this kind involve a common currency, the pyridine nucleotide/flavoprotein/cytochrome chain of electron transfer processes, and the anhydride reactivity of thioesters and phosphoric anhydrides respectively. Some aspects of these processes are considered later; meanwhile the categories illustrated in Figure 1.1 can be taken *seriatim*.

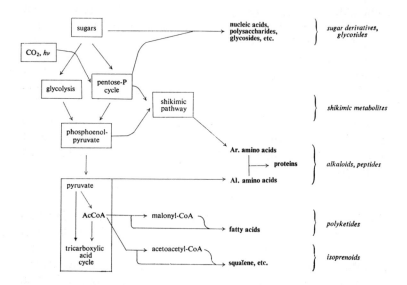

Figure 1.1. *The main flow of carbon metabolism* (*left*), *the main products of primary synthesis* (**bold**), *and the corresponding categories of secondary metabolite* (*italics*).

Sugar conversions

For all organisms the ability to interconvert common sugars is of vital importance. Directly or indirectly, organisms use exogenous or reserve carbohydrates as carbon (and hydrogen) sources; all require the synthesis of structural polysaccharides and the glycosidic coenzymes, nucleic acids, etc. In general, the necessary interconversions and glycosylations involve sugars reacting as their nucleotide esters (e.g. glucose as uridine diphosphoglucose, cytidine diphosphoglucose, etc.). There is a correspondingly widespread category in secondary metabolism. Unfortunately, this cannot be discussed here at any length; it is a largely self-contained field lying rather outside the writer's acquaintance, though it impinges frequently on other topics. In the great range of natural glycosides a variety of sugars, both common and unusual, are found attached to aglycones formed by other secondary pathways. The category includes also such special oligosaccharides as the anti-biotic streptomycins, and might indeed be held to include all the species-specific polysaccharides. In so far as the syntheses of these substances have been investigated, they all seem to involve precisely the same types of sugar nucleotide esters as are seen in the primary processes already noted.

Catabolism of sugars; photosynthesis

The breakdown of sugars is of primary importance, both as an energy-yielding process and as a source of metabolic intermediates. Two pathways are of special prominence (*cf.* Figure 1.1), namely, glycolysis and the "direct" (pentose phosphate cycle) pathway. In glycolysis, hexose phosphate is split hydrolytically to give triose phosphate, which can then be oxidized (*see* below), whereas in the "direct" pathway hexose phosphate is oxidized first, to CO_2 and pentose phosphate; the pentose phosphate may then be utilized as such (for polysaccharide or nucleotide synthesis, etc.), or otherwise it is con-verted by a series of dismutation reactions, the "pentose phosphate cycle", into triose phosphate or—by a reversal of glycolysis—into hexose. In photosynthesis, which provides the carbon intake of green plants, the greater part of the assimilated CO_2 is incorporated by way of intermediates in this same pentose phosphate cycle. All these reactions involve sugar phosphates; the main outlet from the phos-phorylated system is by triose phosphate oxidation through phospho-enolpyruvate.

Now phosphoenolpyruvate is one of the two precursors required for the shikimic/prephenic pathway discussed in Chapter Six; the other is erythrose phosphate, which is a key intermediate in the pentose phosphate dismutation cycle itself. The shikimic pathway, which is primarily used for the synthesis of aromatic amino-acids and related compounds, is thus closely integrated with this phase of sugar metabolism, being related both to the total outflow through phos-phoenolpyruvate and to the pentose phosphate dismutations through erythrose phosphate. Chapter Six and a large part of Chapter Eight are devoted to the secondary metabolites which are likewise formed via shikimic acid. As noted there, such products are particularly important in higher plants, and this probably reflects the close connection with photosynthetic CO_2 assimilation.

Acetyl-CoA and the tricarboxylic acid cycle

In most organisms, further oxidation of triose through phosphoenol-pyruvate and pyruvate leads to acetyl-CoA. This reactive thioester is the main substrate entering the tricarboxylic acid cycle and its variants, which, as an oxidative process, plays a key role in the generation of phosphorylating and reducing agents and is also a source of important metabolic intermediates. Moreover, from acetyl-CoA itself there derive two important pathways of primary biosynthesis, one via malonyl-CoA leading to the fatty acids and one via acetoacetyl-CoA to isoprenoid substances. The secondary metabolites discussed in Chapters Two (polyketides) and Four (isoprenoids) are produced by variations on these two pathways, and with the shikimic acid derivatives they make up the great majority of natural products. Occasionally, intermediates or derivatives from the tricarboxylic acid cycle itself may accumulate as secondary metabolites, and such cases are obviously related.

Amino-acids

Alanine, glutamic acid, and aspartic acid arise directly from tricarboxylic acid cycle intermediates and play especially fundamental roles in nitrogen metabolism, an aspect which has been too little investigated in relation to secondary biosynthesis. Other amino-acids arise less directly but, except for the aromatic amino-acids, all are formed by ways originating in the pyruvate/acetyl-CoA/tricarboxylic acid region of the metabolic network. Pools of all these amino-acids are of course, required for protein synthesis, and Chapter Eight describes some of the very varied range of natural products formed by their secondary metabolism.

C_1 units

The "C_1 pool" of formyl-, hydroxymethyl-, and methyl-derivatives of folic acids is mainly supplied via the amino-acids glycine and serine, and is mainly utilized in primary metabolism for the synthesis of the purine and pyrimidine bases of nucleic acids and coenzymes. As a source of transferrable methyl groups the C_1 pool is also very important in secondary biosynthesis, operating in a way somewhat akin to glycosylation as an auxiliary process in conjunction with other types of synthetic mechanism. Because its function is thus dispersed, a unified account of the role of C_1 units in secondary biosynthesis has not been attempted, though important aspects are noted in several places.

Combination of secondary pathways

Most natural products can be simply assigned to biogenetic groups defined in terms of the types of precursor just listed, but some of the most interesting require the combined operation of several distinct pathways. A good illustration is the antibiotic novobiocin (Figure 1.2),

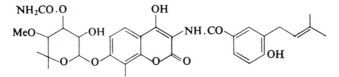

Figure 1.2. *Novobiocin, produced by several converging pathways of secondary biosynthesis.*

in which seven biogenetic units formed by five distinct pathways can be seen, namely:

(*a*) noviose, a sugar formed by rearrangement of glucose with addition of

(*b*) a carbonamido group, derived from an early stage of nitrogen metabolism, and of

(*c*) a C-methyl and an O-methyl group from the C_1 pool; the C_1 pool also furnishes the C-methyl group which is attached to

(*d*) a 3-aminocoumarin derived via tyrosine from shikimic acid; this is also the precursor of the *p*-hydroxybenzoyl group, to which is attached

(*e*) an isopentenyl group derived from mevalonate.

Other examples of such combinations are noted subsequently; they raise interesting questions concerning the order of assembly of the sub-units and the degree of control which may exist to coordinate the contributing processes.

Redox reactions and phosphorylation

As already noted, secondary metabolism is also linked to primary metabolism through redox requirements and phosphorylation requirements, which are not conveniently expressed in a diagram such as Figure 1.1. In primary metabolism, the oxidation-reduction systems are mostly mediated by the two pyridine nucleotide coenzymes, DPN and TPN, and occasionally by flavoprotein, all being linked through a chain of redox exchange reactions to the cytochromes and—in aerobic organisms—the reduction of oxygen. By the process of oxidative

2

phosphorylation this redox chain is also the main source of reactive phosphorylated intermediates generated via adenosine triphosphate, ATP. In photosynthetic organisms the photolytic step can be linked directly to the production of reduced coenzyme (TPNH) and of ATP, independently of CO_2 assimilation. The general pattern of connections between these processes and secondary biosynthesis is therefore of some interest. The availability of reduced coenzymes and the supply of ATP are to a large degree linked by the coupling of redox reactions and phosphorylation in the respiratory chain. However, the existence of the two coenzymes, DPN and TPN, is not irrelevant, for whereas most of the DPNH formed in oxidation reactions is reoxidized by systems coupled to ATP production, most of the TPNH is used directly for synthetic processes. The balance between DPNH-forming and TPNH-forming processes, and in particular between glycolytic and "direct" hexose metabolism, is therefore fundamentally linked to the requirements for phosphorylative and reductive steps in synthetic reactions.

Synthesis of fatty acids and similar reduced polyketides from acetyl-CoA requires ATP, for the generation of malonyl-CoA, and reduced coenzyme, TPNH, whereas in the synthesis of aromatic polyketides the total TPNH requirement is probably small or absent. This difference may well prove to be of importance as a factor regulating the balance between these two types of polyketide synthesis. In contrast, the synthesis of isoprenoids from acetyl-CoA always requires both TPNH and ATP, though, as noted in Chapter Four, the reductive and phosphorylative parts of the sequence are separate. The synthesis of peptides etc. will mainly require ATP, while in alkaloid synthesis no clear requirement for either ATP or reduced coenzymes is apparent—indeed if the process of alkaloid synthesis really begins from the amino-acids themselves, the overall balance of reactions is oxidative. For synthesis in the shikimic/prephenic pathway, a phosphorylation requirement is probably dominant.

Diversification

If, in discovering the common precursors of various categories of natural products, we have detected unifying principles, there yet remains the complementary problem of explaining the actual diversity of the products. At the present time, neither the reasons for this diversity nor the mechanisms by which it is achieved have been satisfactorily elucidated, but from the information so far obtained something of a regular pattern is beginning to emerge. There is a growing number of examples of groups of natural products which appear to arise in a related manner, namely by the synthesis of a specific intermediate product which defines the whole group, and which is then subjected to a variety of reactions selected from a set of relatively non-specific processes. For example, all the regular morphine alkaloids are formed by way of (−)-reticuline, which is synthesized by a specific mechanism and which is then subjected to various reaction steps which, combined in different ways, yield the full variety of products. Several of these diversifying reactions can apparently act on a range of different reticuline metabolites; moreover, many of the same reactions can be observed in the formation of other groups of alkaloids, from intermediates other than reticuline. Very similar situations can be pointed out in quite different categories of natural products and some are noted in the ensuing chapters; in particular, Chapter Six contains a brief analysis of the experimental difficulties caused by these "metabolic grids". If this is the general manner in which the diversity of natural products arises, then some reasons for that diversity can be suggested. We must first presume that the whole process has some function (*see* below); the function of diversification would then be to prevent the accumulation of products whose inhibitory action might be detrimental. It could be that the rather specific initial reactions, such as formation of (−)-reticuline, are generally susceptible to feed-back control by product inhibition; certainly the products of such reactions are usually found only as very minor constituents and seldom accumulate without being chemically modified.

Regulation

As already briefly noted, secondary metabolism is non-essential, at least superficially, and unlike primary metabolism it is not an invariable activity of organisms. Even in unicellular micro-organisms, secondary biosynthesis can usually be associated with a particular phase of the life-cycle; in differentiated multicellular organisms it may occur only in certain parts and at certain times. If we are to understand how the primary and secondary processes are related, we must enquire particularly into the factors responsible for initiating secondary metabolism under certain circumstances, as well as those factors which control secondary metabolism once it has begun. Obviously such problems can be attempted only when the synthetic mechanisms are themselves understood, and since our understanding of these mechanisms is itself a recent development, our understanding of their regulation is even more rudimentary. Most of our present information in these aspects concerns micro-organisms, partly because these are inherently simpler than the higher plants and partly because of the industrial importance of some microbial secondary metabolites. In particular, studies of microbial metabolism allow us to put forward, in very provisional terms, an explanation for the initiation of secondary biosynthesis.

Growth, which in the elementary sense is the replication of cell material, requires the uptake of all the necessary nutrient materials in appropriate proportions. An excessive uptake of any particular nutrient must be reflected in the composition of the cells and, therefore, can occur up to a certain limit only. Under suitable laboratory conditions many micro-organisms can be observed to grow in precisely this replicatory mode with a balanced uptake of nutrients. In the wild state, however, most micro-organisms also need a capacity to adjust to less favourable conditions, since if environmental changes cause even a single nutrient to become limiting, replicatory growth is no longer possible. The most common form of adjustment in response to such circumstances is for replicatory growth to be suspended and for the cells to be transformed, wholly or partly, individually or collectively, into non-replicating resistant structures, which permit survival of the line, possibly with dispersal to new environments. Such changes involve extensive reorganization of metabolic patterns, and apparently this reorganization can include the initiation of secondary biosynthetic activity. In such cases, secondary biosynthesis appears to be a response to the termination of replicatory growth.

In suitable instances it can be shown that the absence of secondary biosynthesis during purely replicatory growth is not due to the absence of appropriate precursors—since, as we have seen, these are already involved in primary metabolic processes—but to the absence of appropriate enzymic activities, and it is the development of these special enzymic capacities which constitutes the initiation of secondary biosynthesis. Now when replicatory growth is halted by some particular unfavourable circumstance, some parts of the primary metabolic network will usually be affected more immediately, and more drastically, than others; an imbalance is thus produced in the system, and this seems to be the immediate cause of the initiation process. Intermediates normally present at low concentrations tend to accumulate temporarily, until the metabolic pressure is relieved by the opening-up of new synthetic pathways. Mechanistically, the initiation and development of secondary biosynthesis is most probably effected by the activation or induction of special enzymes, though this explanation is largely hypothetical. In teleological terms, secondary metabolism would thus appear to provide organisms with a means of adjustment to changing circumstances. The actual *activity* of secondary biosynthesis would be seen as rather more important than the nature of the products formed, and this would at least partly account for their conspicuous diversity.

Such an analysis, which has here been presented in the broadest terms, in fact explains a great many incidental observations of microbial activities and a smaller number of direct studies. It if should prove acceptable in general terms, then we can also see why secondary metabolism should be a feature of higher plants, albeit manifested in a more complex way, because here each cell passes through its own phase of replication and into subsequent non-replicating phases, while all the time it is in an environment which is changing as the entire plant develops. There are a few experimental observations which would accord with this view (but for the complications, *see* Chapter Nine).

As to the factors which may determine the direction to be taken by these new secondary biosyntheses when they are initiated, we remain largely ignorant. Equally, the factors which regulate the intensity of the secondary metabolic processes remain largely unknown, except in the simplest cases where the supply of some particular precursor can be shown to be limiting. All these problems, and many others, remain for the second phase of study.

FURTHER READING

General accounts of primary metabolic processes appear in all textbooks of biochemistry, while specific aspects are regularly reviewed in *Ann. Rev. Biochem.; Adv. Enzymol.*, etc.; particularly useful accounts are:

D. M. Greenberg (ed.), *Metabolic Pathways* (2nd edition; 2 volumes). Academic, New York, 1961.

V. H. Cheldelin, *Metabolic Pathways in Micro-organisms*. Wiley, New York, 1961 (mainly carbohydrate metabolism).

D. Gilmour, *The Metabolism of Insects*. Oliver & Boyd, Edinburgh, 1965 (more generally informative than its title suggests).

A recent compendium with somewhat uneven treatment of both primary and secondary biosynthetic routes is:

P. Bernfeld, *The Biogenesis of Natural Compounds*. Pergamon, Oxford, 1963.

Useful compilations showing the full variety of natural products, with some notes on their biosynthesis, are—

W. Karrer, *Konstitution und Vorkommen der organischen Pflanzen-stoffe*. Birkhauser, Basel, 1959.

M. W. Miller, *The Pfizer Handbook of Microbial Metabolites*. McGraw-Hill, New York, 1961.

The general nature and relationships of secondary metabolites are discussed in:

W. Ruhland (ed.), *Handbuch der Pflanzenphysiologie. X. der Stoffwechsel sekundärer Pflanzenstoffe*. Springer, Berlin, 1958.

T. Swain (ed.), *Chemical Plant Taxonomy*. Academic, New York, 1963.

J. B. Harborne (ed.), *Biochemistry of Phenolic Compounds*. Academic, London, 1964.

J. W. Foster, *Chemical Activities of Fungi*. Academic, New York, 1949 (out of date but still cogent).

J. D. Bu'Lock, *Advances in Applied Microbiology*, 3, 293–342 (1961); J. D. Bu'Lock and A. J. Powell, *Experientia*, **21**, 55 (1965) (microbial products).

Z. Vaněk and Z. Hošťálek (ed.) *Biogenesis of Antibiotic Substances*. Czechoslovak Academy of Sciences (1965) (individual contributions of considerable importance).

The classic exposition of the structure-analytical approach to biogenetic formulations is, of course:

R. Robinson, *The Structural Relations of Natural Products*. Clarendon, Oxford, 1955.

CHAPTER TWO

Polyketides

Polyketides are a large class of natural products grouped together purely on biogenetic grounds; their very diverse structures can all be explained as derived from β-polyketone chains, $—(CH_2CO)_n—$, where the chain is linear and the C_2 units are formally related to acetic acid. Less common, but quite analogous, are chains of "propionate" units $—(CHMe \cdot CO)_n—$. The polyketides include fatty acids, etc. and a very varied series of more complex cyclic compounds, mostly aromatic, and though the type of evidence has varied, the whole group is now seen as a biogenetic unity. Thus, from four C_2 units one can derive, via the formal* intermediate

$$CH_3CO(CH_2CO)_2CH_2CO_2H$$

either octanoic acid (2.1), by reduction, or orsellinic acid (2.2), by aldol condensation. In fact, both the octanoic acid of milk-fat and the orsellinic acid of moulds and lichens are labelled in a manner consistent with this scheme if ^{14}C-acetate is added during their biosynthesis.

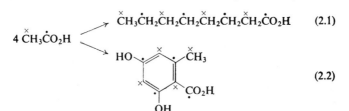

$$\overset{x}{C}H_3\overset{\bullet}{C}H_2\overset{x}{C}H_2\overset{\bullet}{C}H_2\overset{x}{C}H_2\overset{\bullet}{C}H_2\overset{x}{C}H_2\overset{\bullet}{C}O_2H \qquad (2.1)$$

$$4\ \overset{x}{C}H_3\overset{\bullet}{C}O_2H$$

(2.2)

In considering polyketide biogenesis, it is useful to distinguish between (*a*) the *assembly* process, where the C_2 units are linked

---

* In the biosynthesis of the aromatic polyketides, such intermediates may have a real existence, but only as enzyme-bound derivatives, probably of the polyenol, e.g.—

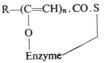

$$R—(C{=}CH)_n . CO . S$$

13

together, (*b*) *modifying* processes, in which the polyketide chain is reduced, cyclized, alkylated, etc., and (*c*) various *secondary* reactions of preformed polyketide derivatives. Also, it is instructive to consider fatty acids first, not only because of the evidence from enzymic studies in this case, but also because the biosynthesis of fatty acids is a general metabolic activity found in all organisms, whereas other types of polyketide are typical "natural products" of very restricted distribution, and may represent individualistic variations on the fatty acid theme.

Biosynthesis of Fatty Acids

(*a*) *Stepwise systems.* The discovery that fatty acids are broken down metabolically by the process of β-oxidation, giving acetyl-CoA,

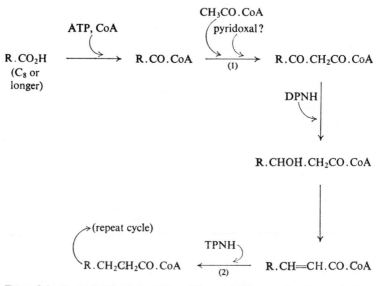

Figure 2.1. *Stepwise chain-extension of fatty acids by acetyl-CoA as a formal reversal of β-oxidation. Detailed mechanisms in steps (1) and (2) differ somewhat from the corresponding reverse steps in β-oxidation.*

provided a plausible mechanism for their synthesis, namely, by reversal of this process. In fact, a synthetic mechanism, which is essentially a reversal of β-oxidation, does exist, though its importance is not general. The initial "Claisen" type of condensation of an acyl-CoA with acetyl-CoA is followed by reduction steps which help to drive the reaction in the synthetic direction (Figure 2.1). Enzyme systems of this type have been found in various organisms, generally in preparations where β-oxidation activity is also concentrated (mitochondria, sarcosomes); their activity seems generally limited to the addition of one or two C_2 units to pre-formed acids with eight or more C atoms. The various reaction steps occur discretely, and it is typical of this kind of system that the addition of labelled acetate gives acids labelled predominantly at the carboxyl end where extension has occurred. Note that the combination of two acetyl-CoA units by this type of mechanism is also the main source of acetoacetyl-CoA in the biosynthesis of isoprenoids (Chapter Four).

(b) "*Malonate*" *systems.* The more widely-distributed mechanism of fatty acid synthesis involves malonyl-CoA as the donor of C_2 units. The "malonate" sequence brings about complete *de novo* synthesis of fatty acids, and the type of mechanism is probably general for polyketide synthesis. The chain-extending agent is malonyl-CoA, a more reactive nucleophile than acetyl-CoA, and decarboxylation helps to drive the reaction in a forward direction. Usually, the malonyl-CoA is formed from acetyl-CoA by a carboxylation reaction, the intermediate CO_2 donor being an enzyme-bound biotin derivative. It is essential to have another acyl-CoA, usually acetyl, which provides the terminal or *starter* unit for the synthesis. The extent to which other acyl-CoA will replace acetyl-CoA as substrates seems to vary from system to system. Sometimes only acetyl-CoA is incorporated into the products, sometimes longer acyl-CoA are incorporated as starters.

In this synthetic sequence, both the starter acetyl-CoA and the malonyl-CoA are separately converted into the corresponding thiolesters of a special carrier protein, in which the reactive centre contains the same β-alanylaminoethanethiol group as coenzyme A. The acetyl-protein and malonyl-protein then react together, liberating one molecule of carrier protein and of CO_2 and forming the acetoacetyl derivative of the carrier protein. Mechanistically this step seems likely to involve, as a preliminary step, transfer of the acetyl group to a thiol group on the enzyme. Subsequent reduction steps convert the acetoacetyl-protein into butyryl-protein, which is then recycled until the C_{16} or C_{18} stage is reached; the free fatty acids are then split off. In the absence of reduction steps acetoacetyl-protein is the main product, and little further reaction occurs. A provisional representation of this rather unusual system is given in Figure 2.2.

Systems of this type usually afford, *in vitro*, mixtures of acids, mainly palmitic. In most organisms the pools of malonyl-CoA and any other free intermediates are quite small, and added ^{14}C-acetate is therefore incorporated with substantial uniformity along the chain; careful observation usually shows slightly higher incorporation in the starter C_2 unit since the malonyl-CoA pool is not entirely negligible. Where finite pools of longer-chain intermediates exist, non-uniform labelling of the malonyl-CoA-derived chain should result, but such a situation has not yet been clearly demonstrated for systems of this kind.

Replacement of the acetyl-CoA starter group by other acyl-CoA, with chain-extension by malonyl-CoA, has been demonstrated for such

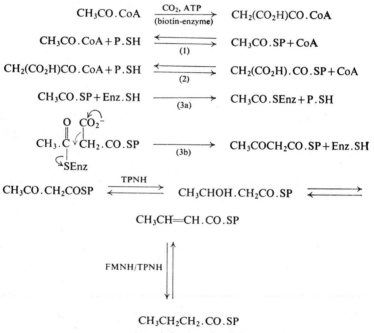

Figure 2.2. *Synthesis of fatty acids by the "malonate pathway". PSH is the acyl-carrier protein. Reactions (1) and (2) involve different enzymes, while (3a) and (3b) are suggested steps in the overall condensation effected by the single enzyme Enz.SH.*

odd-numbered and branched-chain fatty acids as those in Figure 2.3, though the normal enzyme systems react most effectively with acetyl-CoA. Acyl derivatives of intermediate chain-length are also involved as intermediates in the biosynthesis of unsaturated acids (*see* below).

Unsaturated fatty acids

There appear to be several distinct pathways by which the common unsaturated fatty acids are formed, and at the time of writing no clear statement of their relative importance can be offered.

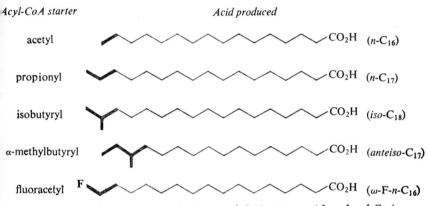

Figure 2.3. Chain-extension of various acyl-CoA starters with malonyl-CoA.

One route involves the aerobic desaturation of preformed acids, possibly as the acyl derivatives of the "carrier" protein used in the synthetic pathway. It is exemplified by the conversion of stearic acid successively into oleic and linoleic acids in yeasts. Less-common enzyme systems may remove hydrogen specifically from other points in the C_{16} or C_{18} chain. Pathways of this kind require the prior synthesis of the corresponding saturated acids and are aerobic (Figure 2.4). This desaturation route, with some variants, is probably the

$$n\text{-}C_{17}H_{35}.CO.SP \xrightarrow{\text{TPNH, O}_2} n\text{-}C_8H_{17}.CH=CH.[CH_2]_7.CO.SP$$

$$\xleftarrow{\text{TPNH, O}_2}$$

$$n\text{-}C_5H_{11}.CH=CH.CH_2.CH=CH.[CH_2]_7.CO.SP$$

Figure 2.4. Aerobic desaturation of long-chain acids as observed in yeasts (PSH = acyl-carrier protein).

most important pathway leading to oleic and other unsaturated fatty acids.

In an alternative mechanism (Figure 2.5), the pathway to oleate diverges from that to palmitate/stearate at the C_{12} stage; here the $\alpha\beta$-unsaturated acid apparently undergoes reduction before chain-building is resumed, whereas the $\beta\gamma$-isomer is homologated without reduction of the double bond. Interconversion of the $\alpha\beta$- and $\beta\gamma$-isomers by way of the β-hydroxyacid provides a controlling mechanism. Pathways of this kind, with malonyl-CoA as the probable source of C_2 units, have been studied in *Clostridium butyricum*, which is an anaerobic micro-organism, in which the oxygen-requiring mechanism of Figure 2.4 would be quite inappropriate. Their importance elsewhere is uncertain.

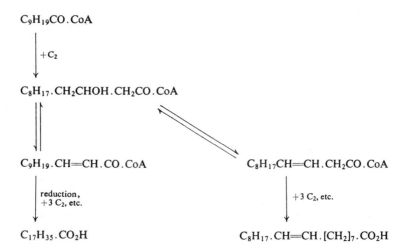

Figure 2.5. Branching pathways to stearic and oleic acids as observed in anaerobic bacteria.

Variant assembly and modifying reactions

Some examples of secondary modifications of fatty acids other than desaturation have been studied. The branched-chain acids of mycobacteria are interesting since they exemplify three quite different ways by which polyketide assembly can lead to branched chains (Figure 2.6). Note particularly that the introduction of methyl groups by secondary alkylation gives a result which is superficially indistinguishable from that obtained by the incorporation of propionate units during assembly. The C-alkylation of polyketides is a very general process (*see* p. 29), whereas the incorporation of propionate, via methylmalonyl-CoA, appears to be particularly characteristic of mycobacteria and their relatives, including streptomycetes. From the latter, in particular, are obtained the various "macrolide" antibiotics, in which the polyketide chains are either wholly propionate-derived,

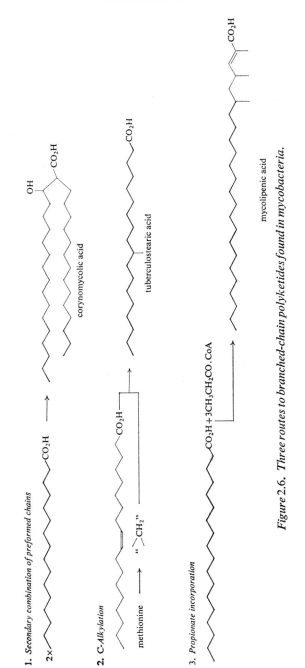

Figure 2.6. Three routes to branched-chain polyketides found in mycobacteria.

as in erythromycin, or of mixed acetate/propionate origin, as in methymycin (Figure 2.7).

In the C-methylated fatty acids of mycobacteria, as in similar steroid derivatives (Chapter Four, p. 65), the methyl group is introduced as $> CH_2$ (derived from the —CH_3 of methionine) and attached to one carbon of a double bond, presumably by some kind of ylid addition reaction followed by reduction. In the lactobacilli a variation of this reaction leads to cyclopropane acids. while in certain plants a corresponding addition to an acetylenic acid may afford cyclopropenes. These alternative mechanisms are noted in Figure 2.8. Certain fatty acids with cyclopentane rings apparently arise from polyunsaturated acids by internal cyclization reactions.

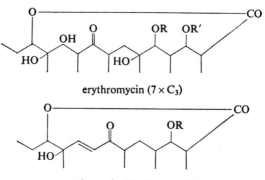

erythromycin ($7 \times C_3$)

methymycin ($5 \times C_3 + 1 \times C_2$)

Figure 2.7. Macrolide antibiotics from Streptomyces formed wholly or largely from "propionate" units (R = desosamine: R' = cladinose).

Polyacetylenes

The natural products with conjugated triple bonds form a distinct class of polyketide, in some respects standing between the fatty acids and the aromatics, since the chain [—C≡C—]$_n$ is at the same oxidation level as a β-polyketone. All the natural polyacetylenes have straight carbon chains, and some, e.g. isanic acid (from a seed-oil), are obviously related to fatty acids; in more complex cases, however, this relationship may be more obscure (Figure 2.9). Tracer experiments show that polyacetylenes are assembled by a malonyl-CoA type of pathway, in which the triple bonds *may* arise by elimination reactions of intermediate enols; good laboratory analogies exist but the enzymic mechanism is uncertain. An alternative mechanism is believed to be involved in the formation of acetylenic derivatives of stearic acid, which might well be precursors of some of the other types of acetylene.

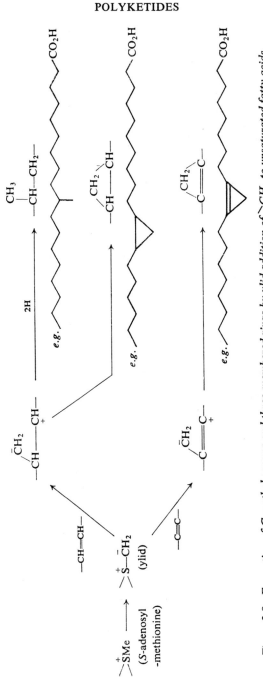

Figure 2.8. *Formation of C-methyl groups and three-membered rings by ylid addition of* $>CH_2$ *to unsaturated fatty acids.*

These C_{18} acids may well be formed by direct desaturation of oleic or other acids—compare the two mechanisms known to be involved in the biosynthesis of ethylenic acids; various chain-shortening reactions might then lead to other types of polyacetylene. In either case, the assembly reaction gives straight-chain polyacetylenic acids, and a variety of well-authenticated further transformations of these are shown in Figure 2.10. As a result of such secondary processes, the final products may be quite complex, and even non-acetylenic (Figure 2.9).

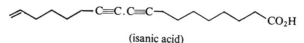

(isanic acid)

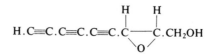

(from *Coprinus* sp.)

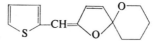

(from *Artemisia* sp., derived from $CH_3 . [C{\equiv}C]_3 [CH{=}CH]_2 CH_2 CH_2 CO_2 H$)

Figure 2.9. *Some natural polyacetylenic compounds.*

(1) $\cdot CH_3 \longrightarrow \cdot CH_2OH \rightleftharpoons \cdot CHO \rightleftharpoons \cdot CO_2H$

(2) $\cdot CH{=}CH . CO_2H \longrightarrow \cdot CH{=}CH_2$ (plants)

(3) $\cdot C{\equiv}C . CO_2H \longrightarrow \cdot C{\equiv}CH$ (fungi)

(4) $\cdot CH{=}CH \cdot \longrightarrow \cdot \underset{\diagdown O \diagup}{CH{-}CH} \cdot \longrightarrow \cdot CHOH . CHOH \cdot$

(5) $\cdot C{\equiv}C . CH_2 \cdot \rightleftharpoons \cdot CH{=}C{=}CH \cdot \rightleftharpoons \cdot CH_2 . C{\equiv}C \cdot$

(6) $\cdot C{\equiv}C . CH{=}CH . CHOH \cdot \longrightarrow$ ⟨furan⟩$-CH_2-$

(7) $\cdot C{\equiv}C . C{\equiv}C \cdot \longrightarrow$ ⟨thiophene⟩

Figure 2.10. *Modifying reactions in the biosynthesis of polyacetylenes, starting from straight-chain acids with conjugated unsaturation.*

Aromatic Polyketides

Biogenetic definition of the aromatic polyketides is due mainly to the work of Birch, by whom a detailed theoretical analysis of the carbon skeletons and oxygenation patterns of known compounds was first combined with an extensive series of tracer incorporation experiments. Whereas the fatty acids include many compounds of completely general occurrence, the aromatic polyketides are all substances of restricted species-distribution, and this may explain why biochemists have neglected their study until quite recently. Nevertheless, the basic mechanisms of assembly and cyclization by which these compounds are formed occur throughout the higher plants and the fungi, and, occasionally, their products have been isolated from animal sources also.

Assembly

Since there is no direct enzymological evidence, it is uncertain how far the processes of chain assembly and of cyclization in polyketide synthesis are really distinguishable. They are, however, conveniently discussed separately, whether as different aspects of a single process or as distinct operations. Structural comparisons (Figure 2.11) suggest that the distinction may be valid, since we find not only examples of the same polyketide chain cyclized in different ways but also examples of analogous cyclization patterns imposed upon quite differently assembled polyketide chains. Moreover in certain mutations of poly-ketide-producing organisms it is possible to obtain impairment of the cyclization step without affecting the nature of the assembly. Examples are given in Figure 2.12.

The assembly process seems to be closely analogous to that in fatty acid synthesis from malonyl-CoA, namely, repeated combination of malonate units, with decarboxylation, and a "starter" which is usually acetyl-CoA. There is, however, the important difference that, whereas in fatty acid synthesis only a limited degree of assembly can occur without reduction of the growing chain, the cyclic unreduced structures of the aromatic polyketides imply that the entire chain is assembled without reduction steps and, therefore, is in a potentially very reactive form. Moreover the *spontaneous* reactions of poly-β-ketones do not lead to aromatic systems of the kind in question. We must therefore conclude that in the biosynthesis of aromatic poly-ketides the assembly is stabilized in some special way not involved in fatty-acid synthesis. If a similar carrier protein is involved, this must carry one or more additional centres that will stabilize the growing assembly and may, ultimately, direct its cyclization. A plausible

3

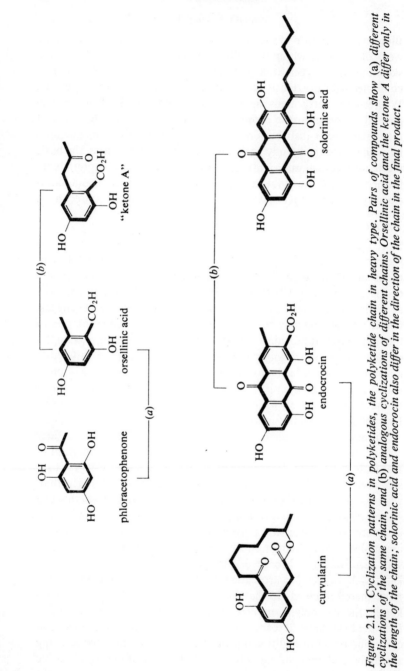

Figure 2.11. Cyclization patterns in polyketides, the polyketide chain in heavy type. Pairs of compounds show (a) different cyclizations of the same chain, and (b) analogous cyclizations of different chains. Orsellinic acid and the ketone A differ only in the length of the chain; solorinic acid and endocrocin also differ in the direction of the chain in the final product.

mechanism involves metal chelates of the poly-enol but has not been verified experimentally.

In tracer experiments, added ^{14}C-acetate is incorporated as acetyl-

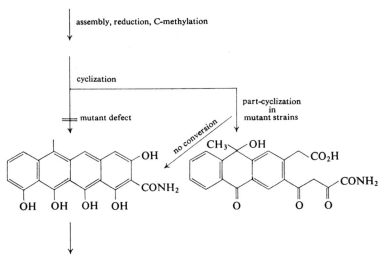

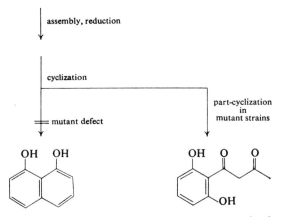

Figure 2.12. *Mutation affecting polyketide cyclization, but leaving assembly unaffected, in* Streptomyces aureofaciens (*above*) *and* Daldinia concentrica (*below*).

CoA, and in normal cases gives substantially equal labelling of the whole chain, with slightly higher incorporation into acetate-derived starter units. Added ^{14}C-malonate is presumed to be incorporated as malonyl-CoA and gives uniform labelling throughout the chain, apart from the starter unit; if this is acetate-derived it is labelled only by that part of the added malonate which has undergone decarboxylation. Figure 2.13 shows the labelling patterns found experimentally in 6-methylsalicylate from *Penicillium* sp. using ^{14}C-acetate and ^{14}C-malonate. The distinction of the starter unit by such observations is sometimes useful in deciding details of biosynthetic mechanism. Thus, in the anthraquinones (Figure 2.14) the pattern of acetate incorporation does not distinguish between the two possibilities that the molecule is formed (*a*) from a single polyketide chain or (*b*) by the combination of two distinct halves; malonate incorporation reveals

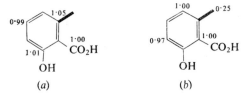

Figure 2.13. *Relative activities in the labelled carbon atoms of 6-methylsalicylic acid produced using* (a) 1-^{14}C-acetate *and* (b) 2-^{14}C-malonate. (*In each case the remaining carbon atoms carry negligible activity.*) *Note the slightly higher activity of the starter group in* (a) *and its markedly lower activity in* (b).

that there is only one starter group, i.e. the molecule is assembled as a single chain. Conversely, the same figure shows the case of rotiorin, in which there are two polyketide chains; one of these is derived from acetoacetate, and it is interesting that malonate is *not* involved in synthesis of this fragment (compare isoprenoid synthesis, Chapter Four). As in fatty acid synthesis from malonate, the C_4 stage in polyketide synthesis involves bound acetoacetate and not the free CoA derivative.

Aromatic polyketides in which the starter group is something other than acetate are exemplified in Figure 2.15. The flavanoids, and other plant products where the starter is an aromatic C_6C_3 acid, form an important group discussed in Chapter Six. In rutilantinone and similar antibiotics from *Streptomyces* the starter is propionate, and in tetracyclines it is a malonate unit (malonamido) which has not undergone decarboxylation. When fungi synthesizing orsellinic acid are supplied with propionate the homologous acid is obtained, so that the requirement for acetyl-CoA is not always inflexible.

Cyclization

As already noted, there is little evidence concerning stages beyond malonyl-CoA in the assembly process: incorporation of C_2 units is generally uniform and potential intermediates with longer chains are

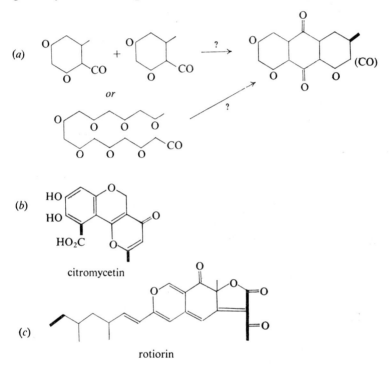

Figure 2.14. *Starter groups (in heavy type) identified by non-incorporation of* ^{14}C-*malonate. In the anthraquinones* (a), *only one starter group is found, favouring the hypothesis of cyclization of a* C_{16} *chain. In citromycetin* (b), *two starter groups, one oxidized, are found. In rotiorin* (c), *neither the* C_2 *starter group nor the attached acetoacetyl group is labelled by* ^{14}C-*malonate.*

not incorporated. Incorporation of the products of impaired cyclization reactions, of the type shown in Figure 2.12, is also not found. The cyclization of the polyketide assembly can be viewed as a stabilization reaction, occurring in a matrix of specific topography which determines the character of the products. Stabilization allows the assembly to be detached from the enzyme on which it hitherto has been bound.

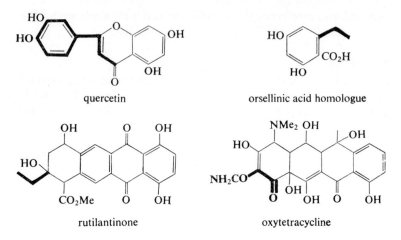

quercetin

orsellinic acid homologue

rutilantinone

oxytetracycline

Figure 2.15. Polyketides in which the starter group (in heavy type) is other than acetate.

Various cyclization patterns in polyketides have already been exemplified and others are shown in Figure 2.16. The ring-closure can involve either terminal acyl or non-terminal carbonyl groups. In substances such as orsellinic acid or alternariol, all the oxygen atoms of the polyketide are apparently retained, except for those involved in

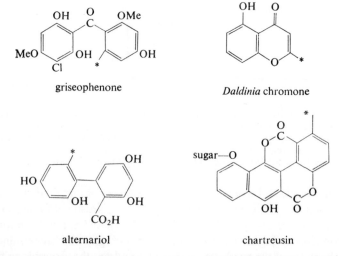

griseophenone

Daldinia chromone

alternariol

chartreusin

*Figure 2.16. Various cyclization patterns of polyketide chains. (The CH₃ terminal is marked *.)*

cyclization steps, and this point has been confirmed experimentally by studies with ^{18}O-acetate. The oxygenation of the alternate carbon atoms around the ring-system is often very distinctive in the final product, and formed part of the original evidence adduced by Birch in support of the "acetate hypothesis". In other compounds, "missing" oxygens imply partial reduction of the polyketide chain: thus, 6-methylsalicylic acid is formed quite analogously to orsellinic acid but with an extra step in which the chain is reduced by TPNH. Such removable oxygen atoms are presumably not required in the biosynthetic processes of stabilizing, folding, or cyclizing the chain; in general, their location accords with this view. There are also compounds in which only part of the polyketide chain is cyclized, the remainder having been stabilized by partial or complete reduction, as in curvularin.

Alkylation reactions

The reduction processes by which "missing" oxygen atoms are removed are most easily understood if they occur before the polyketide chain is stabilized and detached from the enzyme. This may also be true for other modifying reactions, of which some C-alkylations are typical. Many polyketides contain alkyl groups attached to the main chain but not biogenetically part of it, usually methyl, isopentenyl, or polyisoprenoid in nature. Experimentally, it is found that the introduced methyl groups originate from the C_1 pool, and, like O-methyl and N-methyl groups, are labelled by added formate, formaldehyde, or (best) methionine. Introduced isoprenoid groups are labelled by mevalonate (also, of course, by acetate, cf. Chapter Four, but in a different pattern and, generally, at a different dilution from that in the polyketide chain). In Figure 2.17, introduced-isoprenoid groups are seen in auroglaucin and fuscin, and introduced-C-methyl groups in citrinin; in the latter compound, one of the three introduced groups has undergone subsequent oxidation.

The alkylating agents are presumably S-adenosyl-methionine, dimethylallyl pyrophosphate, etc. (Chapter Four), which are electrophilic reagents, and in polyketides the introduced groups are found only on those carbon atoms which would display appropriate reactivity in the polyketone chain, i.e. the alternate enolizable CH_2 groups. Since in the stabilized polyketide these positions would not always show appropriate reactivity, we infer that some of the alkylation reactions can occur before the chain is stabilized. This is confirmed directly by the mutation effects in tetracycline formation, Figure

2.12 and Chapter Seven. The methylation step is here located prior to the release of the first stabilized polyketide from its matrix. However, evidence from other classes of natural products, e.g. Chapter Eight, confirms that electrophilic alkylation of stabilized molecules can also occur.

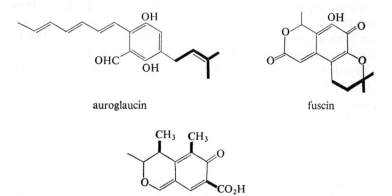

auroglaucin   fuscin

citrinin

Figure 2.17. *Introduced* C_5 *and* C_1 *groups (heavy type) in polyketides from fungi.*

The biosynthesis of tropolones in fungi presents a special case of C-alkylation and ring-enlargement, for which the precursor-incorporation data agree with the scheme shown in Figure 2.18. Another interesting "omnibus" case is that of mycophenolic acid, extensively studied by Birch and co-workers. As shown in Figure 2.19, the aro-

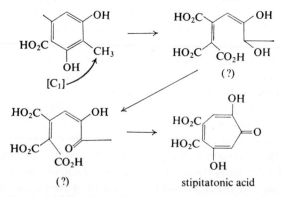

(?)   stipitatonic acid

Figure 2.18. *A model pathway for synthesis of tropolones from alkylated orsellinic acid derivatives. The intermediates are hypothetical (but compare Figure 2.20); the overall pattern is consistent with the observed incorporation of acetate, malonate and formate.*

matic nucleus is that of orsellinic acid, oxidized to the phthalide; methyl groups (from methionine) are attached at $C_{(3)}$ and to phenolic oxygen, while the side-chain at $C_{(5)}$ is derived from mevalonate and represents a geranyl group from which acetone has been removed by oxidation.

Secondary transformations

Where polyketides are modified *after* stabilization it is often possible to isolate the parent compound, or to add it to the system and detect its subsequent transformations; several cases of this kind have been examined. These further reactions of pre-formed compounds are usually simple enzyme processes of well-recognized types, and only a few require special comment. Thus, most of the fungi which synthesize

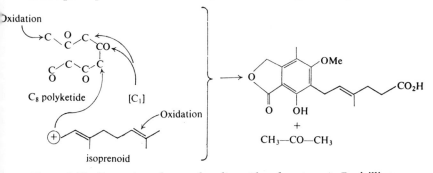

Figure 2.19. Formation of mycophenolic acid and acetone in Penicillium brevicompactum.

6-methylsalicylic acid will effect some or all of the further transformations shown in Figure 2.20. These include oxidation at a benzyl carbon and at nucleophilic sites in the ring, O-methylation, decarboxylation of phenolic acids, quinone formation, and oxidative fission of the benzene ring to give patulin. A similar combination of reactions is involved in the conversion of orsellinic acid into penicillic acid by other fungi (Figure 2.21). This type of ring-opening reaction might be involved as a step in the ring-enlargement by which tropolones are formed, and it has been hypothetically invoked to explain several interesting structural relationships. It is a well-authenticated feature in the breakdown of aromatic substances, by a variety of organisms, but an hypothesis that such a reaction is involved in the biogenesis of certain alkaloids is no longer credited (cf. Chapter Eight).

Other comparatively simple transformations include esterification, halogenation, etc. and need no comment. Combination of pre-formed, polyketide units can occur by esterification, as in depsides, or in more complex ways, of which the most important is the oxidative coupling discussed below. The simultaneous operation of parallel synthetic pathways and a multiplicity of secondary reactions can lead, in practice, to very complex situations, few of which have been pursued

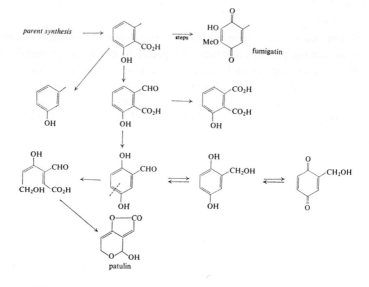

Figure 2.20. *Secondary transformations following synthesis of 6-methyl-salicylic acid by various fungi.*

exhaustively, since the study of such a system requires a combination of experimental methods—sequence observations, precursor-incorporation rates, studies of mutation and reversion, etc. (cf. Chapter Six, p. 83). One system which has been analysed in some detail is that leading from a comparatively simple polyketide to the full complexity of the tetracycline antibiotics. This has been elucidated by mutant studies and precursor-conversion experiments, and is discussed separately in Chapter Seven; as shown in Figure 2.22, the pathway shows multiple branching. This implies that the enzymes catalysing similar steps in the parallel sequences are not wholly specific with

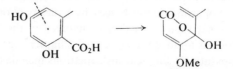

Figure 2.21. *Ring-fission in the conversion of orsellinic acid into penicillic acid.*

9 malonyl-CoA + amide source* + 2H source + methionine-Me†

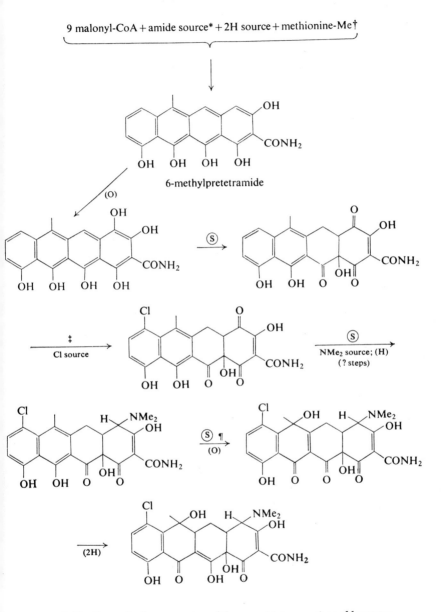

6-methylpretetramide

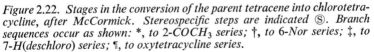

*Figure 2.22. Stages in the conversion of the parent tetracene into chlorotetra-cycline, after McCormick. Stereospecific steps are indicated Ⓢ. Branch sequences occur as shown: *, to 2-COCH₃ series; †, to 6-Nor series; ‡, to 7-H(deschloro) series; ¶, to oxytetracycline series.*

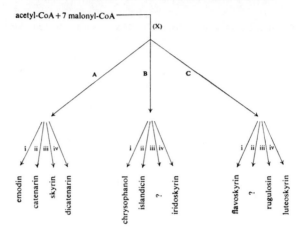

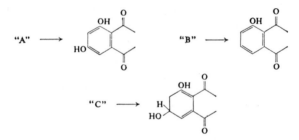

Figure 2.23. Reaction-sequences, part parallel and part competing, in anthra-quinone biosynthesis by P. islandicum strains (after Kikuchi et al.). The three stabilization reactions of the polyketide (X) give the different products:

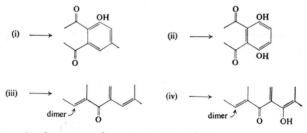

By secondary reactions each of these appears in four types of product:

For example, the main pathway is A (iii), and gives:

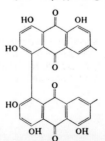

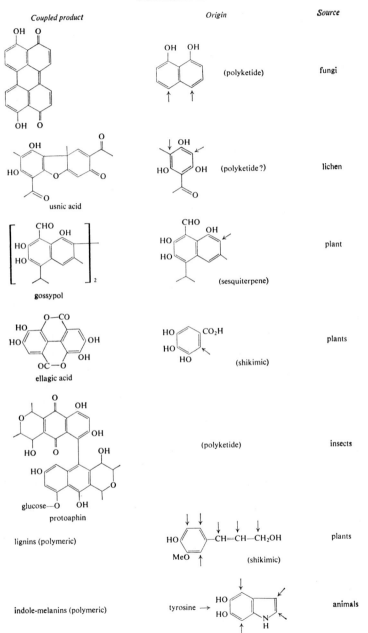

Figure 2.24. Various types of oxidative coupling in phenols of different biogenetic origins (positions of coupling shown by arrows).

respect to their substrates. On the other hand, they are entirely responsible for the detailed stereochemistry of the products (since the parent polyketides are planar molecules); i.e. they effect fully stereospecific reactions.

A fairly complete analysis of another system is summarized in Figure 2.23, based mainly on the work of Kikuchi *et al.* on the anthraquinones of *Penicillium islandicum*. Here there are three basic oxidation patterns in the stabilized polyketide chain, and each product may be subjected to four competing types of secondary reaction; various combinations of these occur in different strains of the fungus.

Note on Oxidative Coupling

The oxidative coupling of phenols is an important biosynthetic process conveniently discussed here, although it also occurs with phenols which are not polyketides, several examples of which will be encountered in later sections. A number of enzyme systems will bring about one-electron oxidation of phenols followed by radical coupling; such reactions are also effected by reagents like ferric chloride but *in vivo* systems may show far greater specificity. Since phenoxy radicals are tautomeric, they can combine in various ways, by C—C and C—O bonds and (in suitable cases) by intra- as well as inter-molecular coupling.* The subject has been exhaustively reviewed (p. 37) and several elegant laboratory syntheses have been modelled on biosynthetic reactions of this kind. Besides leading to natural products of defined structure, oxidative coupling also affords various important polymers, including lignins, melanins, certain tannins, etc. No adequate discussion of this very wide field is possible here, but in Figure 2.24 various examples are collected. These are intended to show a variety of types of C—C and C—O coupling, intermolecular dimerization and intramolecular cyclization, etc., also to illustrate how the process is found in a wide range of organisms and involves phenols of various biogenetic origins. Other examples will be found in Chapters Six and Eight.

FURTHER READING

General

J. H. Richards and J. B. Hendrickson, *The Biosynthesis of Steroids, Terpenes, and Acetogenins*. Benjamin, New York, 1964 (acetogenins≃polyketides).

* It is generally uncertain whether coupling occurs by pairing of radicals or by radical attack on unchanged phenol, but the former mechanism seems most likely *in vivo*.

Fatty acids etc.

S. J. Wakil, *Ann. Rev. Biochem.*, **31**, 369–406 (1962).

R. Vagelos, ibid., **33**, (1964).

J. D. Bu'Lock, *Progress in Organic Chemistry*, **6**, 86–134 (1964) (polyacetylenes).

Aromatic polyketides

A. J. Birch and F. W. Donovan, *Australian J. Chem.*, **6**, 360–368 (1953) (the original acetate hypothesis).

A. J. Birch, *Proc. chem. Soc.*, 1962, 3–13.

R. W. Rickards in W. D. Ollis (ed.) *Chemistry of Natural Phenolic Compounds*. Pergamon, Oxford, 1961, pp. 1–19.

R. Bentley, *Ann. Rev. Biochem.*, **31**, 589–624 (1962).

A. C. Neish, in J. H. Harborne (ed.), *Biochemistry of Phenolic Compounds*. Academic, London, 1964, pp. 295–360.

Articles by C. H. Hassall, J. R. D. McCormick (tetracyclines), J. W. Corcoran (macrolides), S. W. Tanenbaum and S. Gatenbeck in Z. Vaněk and Z. Hošťálek, *Biogenesis of Antibiotic Substances*. Czechoslovak Academy of Sciences, Prague 1965.

Oxidative coupling

D. H. R. Barton and T. Cohen, in *Festschrift A. Stoll*, Birkhauser, Basel, 1957, pp. 117–143.

H. Erdtman and C. E. Wachtmeister, ibid., pp. 144–165.

C. H. Hassall and A. I. Scott, in W. D. Ollis (ed.), *Chemistry of Natural Phenolic Compounds*. Pergamon, Oxford, 1961, pp. 119–133.

CHAPTER THREE

Precursor-Incorporation Experiments in Fungi—Design and Interpretation

The Experimental Material. Fungi are capable of producing a great variety of metabolites in good yields, growing quite quickly on laboratory media, and have proved very convenient for tests of biogenetic hypotheses. Their use in surface cultures requires virtually no special equipment save an incubator-room and a sterilizer, but as a general rule submerged cultures, which require either a shaking-machine or a set of agitated fermentors, are preferred for their higher metabolic activity and more uniform behaviour. Shake or surface cultures can be grown in 500–750 ml conical flasks, and for large-scale experiments it is better to increase the number of flasks than to use larger volumes, though this requires a standardized procedure for building up the inocula. The greatest disadvantage of fungi is their tendency to lose or change metabolic capabilities (usually half-way through a research programme!). Such changes are accelerated by repeated sub-culturing of the parent stock, and when a good parent strain has been obtained (ideally by fresh isolation from natural sources but usually by borrowing from another laboratory), its deterioration can fortunately be minimized by storing slopes under oil or quartz sand at 4° C, when they will keep for a year or more.

Having set up the cultures in this way, and being provided with some efficient method of isolating the required metabolite, the next step in a biosynthetic study is a matter for careful experimental design. The basic features of this problem are common to all biogenetic studies by this method and are not always fully appreciated, consequently some space is devoted here to their analysis.

A Model Cell. For illustrative purposes we shall use the simplified "model cell" shown in Figure 3.1. Here A_0 is the food supply (carbon source) while A, B, C, and many other compounds not shown, are the normal cell components linked by a complex network of reactions. The sequence from C to the extracellular products S_0 and U_0 is the special biosynthetic pathway under study.

The " permeability " of fungi to substances in the external medium is much less selective than that of many higher organisms—another experimental convenience—but nevertheless, some substances can enter the cells far more readily than others. Moreover, substances from outside the cell often must undergo special reactions before they enter the metabolic network. For example, the situation shown for C, C_0, C_0' in Figure 3.1 is typical of "malonate" in many Penicillia: free malonic acid (C_0') does not enter the cells, while diethylmalonate (C_0) does, but the ester requires hydrolysis and conversion into malonyl-CoA (C) before it is metabolically active. The double requirement, for

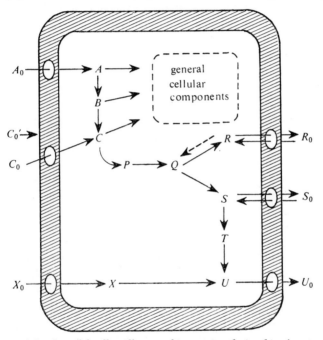

Figure 3.1. *A model cell to illustrate biogenetic relationships* (see *text*).

free entry and for "activation", is an important one, and is particularly critical for highly polar or unusually complex substrates. It applies equally critically in studies of mutant micro-organisms, as discussed in Chapter Seven. Unfortunately, it has proved difficult to obtain biosynthetically active preparations from disrupted fungal cells, in which the permeability effects might be avoided.

Figure 3.1 also serves to show how the widely-used term "precursor" might be applied to substances of very different status. For example, the substances A_0, A, and B are all "precursors" of U_0, but the usage is hardly informative—A_0 and A are precursors of all the cell contents! Substance C is a precursor in the distinctive sense that it is the last compound in the general metabolic network which is also in the special biosynthetic sequence, and the term "prime precursor" is useful for such a case; if the existence of C were undiscovered, this designation would apply to B. The substances P, Q, S, T are peculiar to the special pathway and are more usefully called "intermediates"; note that S appears outside the cells as S_0, which may not be identical with S. Substance R is an alternative metabolite of intermediate Q, and if R is formed reversibly it may appear to function as an intermediate. Substance X is an artefact, produced only when X_0 is added but convertible into U, U_0; like R, it is liable to be diagnosed as an intermediate.

In general, the identification of precursors in intact cells can involve studies either of (a) the efficiency, or (b) the specificity, of conversion into a product. Ideally, both aspects should be studied, though in practice one or other dominates the experimental design, and in tracer studies the two are complementary.

Efficiency of precursor conversion

In Figure 3.1, we might identify the prime precursor C as being that normal cell component of which the highest proportion is converted into metabolites S_0, U_0.* Unfortunately, the experimental measurement of conversion efficiency presents several difficulties. Figure 3.2 shows the general course of mould metabolism in a very typical case, where the mould utilizes substrate A_0 for cell growth (dry weight curve) and, at a certain stage of development, produces metabolites like S_0 and U_0 of Figure 3.1. In any such situation, it is clear that:

(a) much of the nutrient A_0 is consumed before synthesis of S_0 or U_0 begins, so that expressing yields as a proportion of the A_0 supplied or consumed up to a certain time is misleading;

(b) variations in the details of Figure 3.2, such as may occur with different substrates, make comparisons "under standard conditions" difficult;

(c) the concentration of S_0 at any time is a function of past rates of synthesis and of further metabolism, and never measures the amount

---

* In the author's experience with fungi, a cell-component of very general importance, entering into a number of metabolic processes (like acetyl-CoA), shows *ca.* 2–20 per cent conversion into end-product metabolites, and more specialized components like methionine some 20–70 per cent; lower apparent conversions usually merit further study.

of S_0 which has been formed; conversely the " yield" of U_0 is dependent on the amount of S_0 which has accumulated.

Such ambiguities are removed, if the general course of events is understood, by studying *rates* of conversion. If at some specified time the total rate of accumulation of $(S_0 + U_0)$ is measured, this can be compared with the current rate of substrate utilization.

When the conversion of different substrates is to be compared, it is necessary to assume (or to show) that the general balance of cellular reactions is not disturbed by the change of substrate. Thus, in Figure 3.1, if we substitute C_0 for A_0 as carbon source, the conversion into U_0 will be increased only if the proportions of substance C undergoing

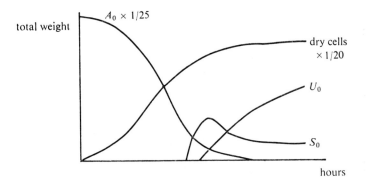

Figure 3.2. *Course of a typical fermentation, with carbon source* (A_0) *used for synthesis of cell material* (*dry cells*) *and metabolites* (S_0 *and* U_0). *See Figure* 3.1.

various reactions are not significantly changed. For example, C_0 might be malonic acid and C malonyl-CoA; substitution of C_0 for A_0 might then give an increased yield of some polyketide (U_0), but other possibilities are:

(*a*) the cells might die, or continue metabolism at a reduced rate;
(*b*) since malonate inhibits succinoxidase, succinic acid or other metabolites from endogenous sources might accumulate;
(*c*) for the same reason, synthesis of a metabolite requiring ATP or reduced coenzymes normally afforded by the citrate cycle might be inhibited irrespective of precursor relationships;
(*d*) in their new environment the cells may develop new synthetic capacities not previously present.

To avoid the effects of a gross change of substrate, the main carbon source is frequently left unchanged and various supplementary substrates are added. If these are used in small amounts, the balance is less seriously disturbed, but at the same time the observable effects are diminished. However, the use of isotopically labelled substrates enables these to be added in very small (tracer) amounts, which are usually insufficient to disturb the metabolic balance*, and the substrate conversion can then be measured radiochemically.

Tracer incorporation from labelled substrates

It is desirable to measure the degree of conversion of a tracer substrate even when the main aim of an experiment is to establish the specificity of substrate incorporation, as discussed later. The full analysis of precursor-incorporation data can be quite complex—a good account is given by Aronoff (*see* bibliography, p. 45)—and rigorous study requires rather more detailed information than is usually available in biogenetic studies, but the major qualitative effects can be shown more simply. Suppose that, in Figure 3.1, A_0 is the main carbon source and C_0* is a labelled substrate, added in tracer amount and entering the cell freely. When C_0* is added, the radioactivity of C will rise sharply, and then fall (exponentially) as fresh C is synthesized from A_0. Reference to Figure 3.2 shows that if C_0* is added too early, the radioactivity of C may be dissipated before synthesis of U_0 has begun; for this reason, tracer should not be added until the pathway under study is known to be operating. Then, if we examine an end-product like U_0, the *total* radioactivity (specific activity × weight) will rise to a limit representing the proportion of the total turnover of C used for this synthesis. The *specific* activity of U_0 will pass through a maximum. If, however, we examine a product liable to further metabolism, like S_0, the *total* activity in S_0 will also pass through a maximum and then fall as the labelling is "washed out" by fresh material; eventually the end-product U_0 will be *more* active than the intermediate S_0(!).

In general, therefore, we require information as to how the metabolites accumulate during the experiment, and must be sufficiently well-informed to add the tracer substrate at an appropriate time. If the metabolite in question is an end-product, the experiment can then be allowed to proceed "indefinitely", and the radioactivity in the total product is then expressed as a fraction of that supplied in the precursor. For a transient metabolite like S_0 a short incorporation time is

* This is the standard assumption, and tracer substrates should always be added at the highest available specific activity for this reason. In delicately-balanced systems the assumption may still be unjustified; this is also the case when the cell component corresponding to the tracer substrate is present in very small amounts (e.g. biotin).

necessary; extra experimental work is then required, and the most satisfactory simple expression of the results is to give the rate at which radioactivity first appears in the metabolite as a fraction of the corresponding rate of disappearance of labelled precursor.

An important auxiliary method is to use metabolites of known biosynthetic origin as "internal references". For example, in a metabolite suspected of being either a polyketide or a phenylpropane derivative, we might supply various tracer substrates and in each case isolate, say, fatty acid, triterpenoid, poly-saccharide, and tyrosine from the cells, as well as the metabolite in question. Incorporation into the metabolite can then be compared qualitatively with the general pattern of biosynthetic activity; the method is a powerful one, though still subject to some of the difficulties of experimental design and interpretation outlined above. An obvious variant arises when different parts of the molecule in a single metabolite are formed from different precursors (e.g. mycophenolic acid, Figure 2.19, p. 31).

Specificity of precursor incorporation

The most powerful single method in biogenetic studies is to supply tracer amounts of a precursor, isotopically labelled in a recognizable pattern, then to isolate the labelled metabolite and degrade it so as to reveal a labelling distribution in which the precursor units can be recognized. Success depends on the correct choice of labelled precursor, effective incorporation conditions, and truly selective degradation of the metabolite. The selectivity of the degradation methods used is of supreme importance but needs little discussion here: requirements are for reactions which proceed "cleanly" by known mechanisms, and for careful bench-work, and some leading references are included in the bibliography. In some special circumstances it may be necessary to use substantially-enriched heavy isotope substrates (e.g. ^2H, ^{13}C) rather than radioactive isotopes (an example will be found in Chapter Five), and analytical methods must be somewhat differently designed. The general conditions required for effective precursor incorporation have already been noted.

The labelled precursor must be a compound which can enter the cells, and it is desirable that the main outlines of its metabolism should be known. This is important in deciding whether the observed incorporation efficiency is significant (cf. footnote, p. 40), also in choosing the pattern of labelling in the precursor, since this pattern must be distinctively recognizable in the product. Failures in this respect are the most common causes of incorrect deductions from this type of experiment. For example, many ^{14}C-labelled substrates will afford some $^{14}CO_2$, which can partly be assimilated into sugars and thence into a variety of cell substances. Substrates such as pyruvate, formate, and even acetate, can contribute ^{14}C by devious routes into all manner of metabolites; the partial randomization of 2-[^{14}C]-acetate by re-cycling in the citrate cycle is a well-known phenomenon. More specific reactions can also be misleading, e.g. the formation of serine from the side-chain of tryptophane, and thence incorporation via the C_1 pool,

1st Data

$C_7H_{15} \cdot \overset{*}{C}O_2H$ added to cells $\rightarrow C_8H_{17} \cdot CH{=}CH \cdot CH_2 \cdot \overset{*}{C}O_2H$, 5 per cent total ^{14}C used, 95 per cent of this in $C_{(1)}$.

1st Conclusion

$C_{(1)}$–$C_{(8)}$ of the C_{12} acid derive from the C_8 acid added, by chain-extension at the methyl end.

Query

Fatty acids are metabolically labile; also the conversion of ^{14}C into product (5 per cent) seems rather low.

Further data

(1) 7-^{14}C-octanoate also gives mainly 1-^{14}C-dodecenoate in similar experiment; so does 1-^{14}C-acetate.

(2) 1-^{14}C-decanoate used similarly gives 60 per cent conversion into 3-^{14}C-dode-canoate.

Conclusion

By β-oxidation the octanoic acid generates ^{14}C-acetate; the cells contain endo-genous acetyl-CoA and decanoyl-CoA, which react thus:

$$C_9H_{19}\overset{o}{C}O \cdot CoA + CH_3\overset{*}{C}O \cdot CoA \rightarrow C_8H_{17} \cdot CH{=}\overset{o}{C}H \cdot CH_2 \cdot \overset{*}{C}O \cdot CoA.$$

Figure 3.3. *Hypothetical illustration of a spurious result from incorporation experiments.*

or the breakdown of fatty acids and a wide variety of other substances into specifically-labelled acetyl-CoA, which can then be used for other syntheses. It is kinder to illustrate such pitfalls by a hypothetical example (Figure 3.3).

Where difficulties of this kind are acute, it may be possible to use a doubly-labelled precursor to establish the intact incorporation of a particular unit. A classic example is the use of $^{14}CD_3$-derivatives to establish intact transfer of methyl groups, or of a [^{14}C, ^{15}N]-labelled amino-acid; the test is that both isotopes are incorporated with com-parable dilution in short-term experiments.

FURTHER READING

General

S. Aronoff, *Techniques of Radiobiochemistry*. Iowa State University, Ames, 1960.

V. W. Cochrane, *Physiology of Fungi*. Wiley, New York, 1958.

D. Perlman, A. P. Bayan and N. A. Giuffre, *Advances in Applied Microbiology*, **6**, 27–68 (1964).

Typical experiments

A. J. Birch, R. A. Massy-Westropp, R. W. Rickards and H. Smith, *J. Chem. Soc.*, **1958**, 360 (^{14}C-griseofulvin).

S. Gatenbeck and K. Mosbach, *Acta chem. Scand.*, **13**, 1561 (1959). (^{18}O-orsellinic acid).

R. Bentley and J. G. Keil, *J. Biol. Chem.*, **237**, 867 (1962). [^{14}C-penicillic acid from a range of substrates).

CHAPTER FOUR

Isoprenoids

A biogenetic definition of isoprenoid compounds developed relatively early, and Ruzicka has given an interesting historical account (*see* p. 69). Though the majority of natural terpenes can be built up, on paper, from "isoprene units",

$$\begin{array}{c} -\text{C}-\text{C}-\text{C}-\text{C}- \\ | \\ \text{C} \end{array}$$

, exceptions were soon noted; it was the recognition that even these irregular structures could arise by rational rearrangements of regular polyisoprenes that provided a basis for the "biogenetic isoprene rule". Characteristically, such considerations provided a useful unifying theory but did not lead to identifications of biosynthetic precursors.

Meanwhile the origin of cholesterol had received biochemical attention; the derivation from acetate had been studied and a relationship to a triterpene (squalene) was eventually suspected. The characteristic isoprenoid precursors proved elusive until, coincidentally, mevalonic acid was identified as an acetate-replacing factor for certain mutant bacteria. From this point onwards there was a rapid convergence of chemical, biogenetic, and enzymological studies, particularly associated with the work of Bloch Cornforth and Lynen.

In discussing the biogenesis of isoprenoids we shall consider, first, the origin of isoprene units and their polymerization, and, second, the cyclization and other reactions of polyisoprene chains. Such a separation is biochemically sound and forms an interesting comparison with that attempted for polyketides in Chapter Two. Mechanistically, isoprenoid synthesis has three phases—synthesis of mevalonate from thiol esters, formation of polyisoprene chains via phosphate derivatives, and cyclization.

Formation of Polyisoprene Chains

Biosynthesis of mevalonate

Routes to mevalonic acid from acetyl-CoA and from leucine are summarized in Figure 4.1. The thiol esters of acetic, acetoacetic, and β-hydroxy-β-methylglutaric acids are normally interconvertible, and mevalonate synthesis is controlled by the reduction of hydroxy-methylglutaryl-CoA. This reduction requires two molecules of TPNH and is virtually irreversible.

The route from leucine is usually less important. The key step is the biotin-dependent carboxylation of senecioyl-CoA (compare malonyl-CoA synthesis); though the carbon atom thus added is that which is eventually lost in forming isoprene units, some CO_2 can become

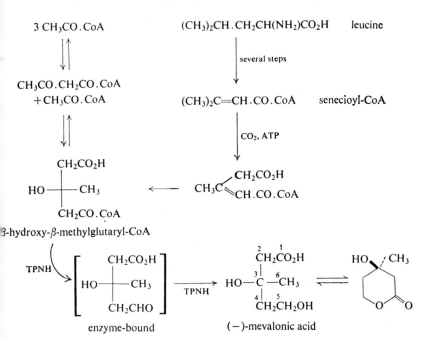

Figure 4.1. *The biosynthesis of mevalonate.*

incorporated because of the cycling between acetyl- and hydroxy-methylglutaryl-CoA.

Since free acetoacetyl-CoA is not normally an intermediate in polyketide synthesis (Chapter Two), the paths from acetyl-CoA to polyketides and isoprenoids diverge at this early stage. The balance between these important biosynthetic pathways is at least partly controlled by two reactions: on the one hand, the carboxylation of acetyl-CoA, and on the other, the reduction of hydroxymethyl-glutaryl-CoA.

The C$_5$ pyrophosphates

Figure 4.2 continues the sequence. Two successive phosphorylations afford the pyrophosphate of mevalonic acid, and the product of a third phosphorylation undergoes concerted elimination and decarboxylation to yield the Δ^3-isopentenyl pyrophosphate as shown. By proton rearrangement this yields 3,3-dimethylallyl pyrophosphate, which is the active alkylating agent in isoprenoid biosynthesis and the biological form of the biogenetic "isoprene unit".

The stereochemistry of these reactions is, of course, under full enzymic control; note in particular that $C_{(2)}$ of mevalonate furnishes, specifically, the methylene group of isopentenyl pyrophosphate and

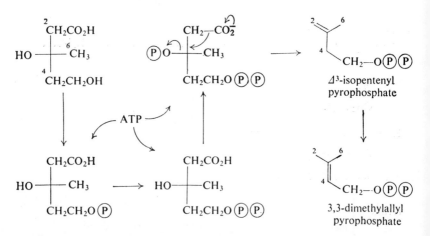

Figure 4.2. *Conversion of mevalonate into the C$_5$ pyrophosphates; the numbering is that of the mevalonic acid, from which $C_{(1)}$ is lost.*

the *trans*-methyl group of dimethylallyl pyrophosphate. Mevalonate labelled at $C_{(2)}$ is frequently employed in tracer experiments, and this allows observations of the distinction between $C_{(2)}$ and $C_{(6)}$ of mevalonate in certain critical cases.

Alkylation of non-isoprenoids

As an allylic ester, 3,3-dimethylallyl pyrophosphate or the derived cation is an effective electrophilic alkylating agent. It is presumably the precursor of the mevalonate-derived isopentenyl groups which appear in many natural products, attached to non-terpenoid units at positions susceptible to electrophilic attack—phenolic oxygen, activated methylene, nucleophilic sites on aromatic rings, etc.

Similarly, higher isoprenoids reacting as allylic pyrophosphates may attach polyisoprene residues. Examples are seen in Figure 4.3 and elsewhere in this book. The intimate mechanism of these alkylations is

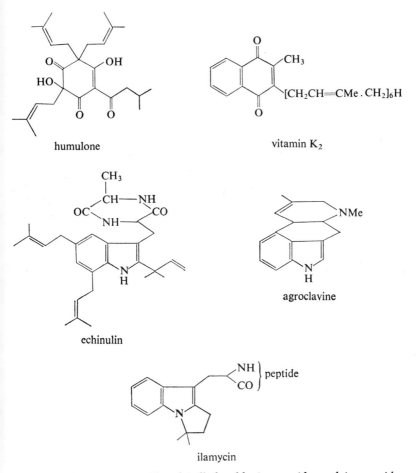

Figure 4.3. *Non-isoprenoid nuclei alkylated by isoprenoid or polyisoprenoid groups, presumably via electrophilic attack (in Vitamin K$_2$ this would involve attack on the quinol).*

not known, but they are clearly controlled by specific enzymes—see, for example, the three differently alkylated indoles which can be compared in Figure 4.3.

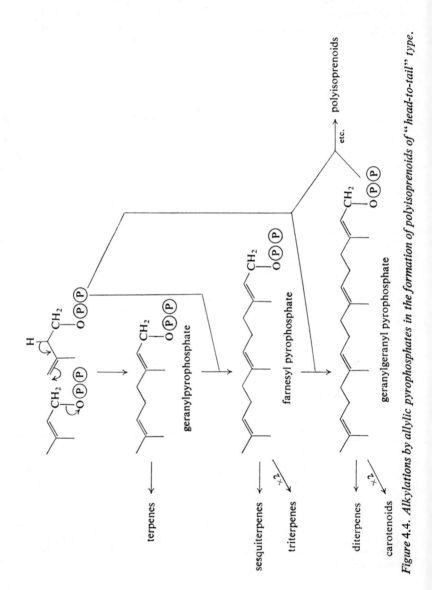

Figure 4.4. *Alkylations by allylic pyrophosphates in the formation of polyisoprenoids of "head-to-tail" type.*

Alkylation-polymerization of isoprenoids

Alkylation by dimethylallyl pyrophosphate is also the means by which polyisoprenoids are built up. As shown in Figure 4.4, the C_{10} terpenes arise thus by alkylation of the precursor isopentenyl pyrophosphate. In the process the double bond of the second C_5 unit migrates as shown (probably with assistance of the neighbouring phosphate group),

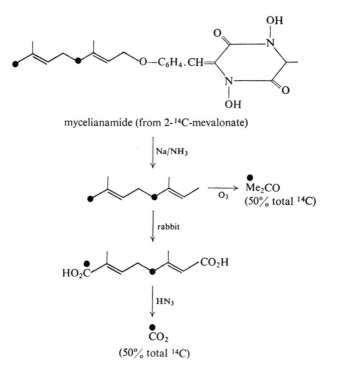

mycelianamide (from 2-^{14}C-mevalonate)

Me$_2$CO
(50% total ^{14}C)

CO$_2$
(50% total ^{14}C)

Figure 4.5. Proof of steric differentiation in the gem-*dimethyl group of geraniol synthesized from* 2-^{14}C-*mevalonate.*

giving geranyl pyrophosphate; since this is an allylic ester, the process can be repeated, generating C_{15} (farnesyl) and C_{20} (geranylgeranyl) chains. In the formation of rubber this polymerization proceeds indefinitely, with allylic centres on the growing latex particles and isopentenyl pyrophosphate in the aqueous phase.* Considerable repetition of the alkylation step also occurs in forming the isoprenoid side-chains

* In forming the rubber polymer, the migrating double bonds take up the exceptional *cis*-configuration by stereospecific proton removal.

in ubiquinones, plastoquinones (vitamins K), and certain other compounds. With these exceptions, the polymerization ends at the C_{10}, C_{15}, or C_{20} stage and the products are precursors of the mono-, sesqui-, and diterpenes respectively, all with "head-to-tail" linkages of isoprene units. The carbon chains of triterpenes (C_{30}) and carotenoids (C_{40}) arise by further steps discussed below.

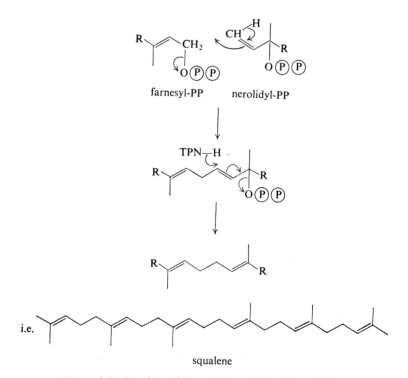

Figure 4.6. *Coupling of C_{15} units in squalene biosynthesis.*

As a consequence of the stereospecificity already mentioned, note that in the polyisoprenoids $C_{(2)}$ of mevalonate now appears as the *trans*-methyl of the isopropylidene end-group and in no other C-methyl groups. Some experimental tests of this are noted later, but a particularly direct proof for the geranyl group of mycelianamide is shown in Figure 4.5. Here half the total ^{14}C is in the isopropylidene group; Birch and co-workers used the stereospecific oxidation of methylgeraniolene by rabbits to prove the localization of this ^{14}C, as shown.

"Tail-to-tail" linkages

The C_{30} chain of triterpenes and the C_{40} chain of carotenoids are symmetrical, with a central "tail-to-tail" linkage between two "head-to-tail" chains. The coupling reaction in the triterpene series has been elegantly studied by Cornforth and is outlined in Figure 4.6. Allylic rearrangement of farnesyl pyrophosphate produces the nerolidyl derivative, with a terminal double bond which can now be alkylated by a second molecule of farnesyl pyrophosphate. The final dephosphorylation is reductive, using a stereospecific displacement by hydride ion from TPNH. The product is squalene, parent substance of the triterpenes and their degradation products, the steroids.

The corresponding C_{20}, C_{20} coupling leading to carotenoids has not been so successfuly elucidated. At present, the most generally agreed view is that the coupling product is phytoene, $C_{40}H_{64}$, with a double bond in the central position. This implies a different mechanism to that in squalene synthesis, and a possible scheme is shown in Figure 4.7.

Cyclization etc. of Polyisoprene Chains

The polyisoprenoid pyrophosphates can be decomposed hydrolytically, giving the corresponding primary alcohols (e.g. geraniol) or their allylic isomers (e.g. linalool). Alternatively, they may generate allylic cations which can act as alkylating agents, either intermolecularly, as already described, or intramolecularly, i.e. by cyclization. The carbonium ions generated in the intramolecular reactions may also be susceptible to rearrangements of the Wagner-Meerwein type. It has been the particular contribution of Ruzicka and his school, at a time when chemical and stereochemical understanding of the cyclic isoprenoids was developing rapidly, to set out in detail the hypothesis that complex isoprenoids are generated by stereospecific carbonium alkylation and rearrangement reactions of the folded polyisoprene chain; the most important validation of this hypothesis is its entire success as a structural and stereochemical generalization. The examples which follow are some of those which have been studied experimentally, and which often supply confirmation of particular details.

Monoterpenes

Several of the relatively simple terpenes have been shown to incorporate $2\text{-}^{14}C$-mevalonate in the expected manner, and some are shown in Figure 4.8. Apart from the geranyl group in mycelianamide, already discussed, the stereochemical implications have not been explored, but the type of mechanism shown provides a satisfactory structural

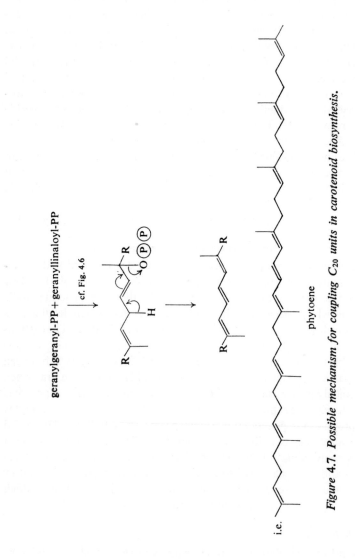

Figure 4.7. Possible mechanism for coupling C_{20} units in carotenoid biosynthesis.

hypothesis. Geranyl pyrophosphate is the presumed precursor, but this has not been proved directly.

Sesquiterpenes

The very complex series of natural sesquiterpenes is believed to arise from farnesyl pyrophosphate, and some examples have been studied by tracer methods which clarify details concerning rearrangement

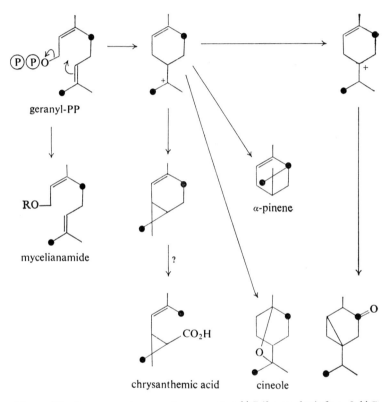

geranyl-PP

mycelianamide

α-pinene

chrysanthemic acid   cineole

Figure 4.8. *Some monoterpenes incorporating* [14]*C* (*heavy dots*) *from* 2-[14]*C-mevalonate; only in the case of mycelianamide is the* steric *location of labelling known experimentally.*

steps etc. Three such cases are outlined in Figure 4.9, starting from (*a*), the allylic farnesyl cation. One mode of cyclization gives (*b*), probably the parent substance of the bisabolene-type sesquiterpenes, which, by further cyclization and the double 1,2-shift of methyl groups, affords the carbon skeleton of trichothecolone, a fungal product. Here,

5

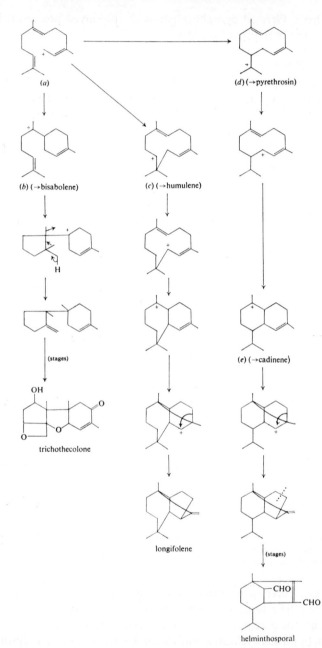

(a)

(d) (→pyrethrosin)

(b) (→bisabolene)

(c) (→humulene)

H

(stages)

trichothecolone

longifolene

(e) (→cadinene)

(stages)

helminthosporal

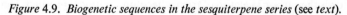

Figure 4.9. Biogenetic sequences in the sesquiterpene series (see text).

isotope data confirmed the double nature of the rearrangement, and the stereochemistry of the product is consistent with this scheme. An alternative cyclization of (*a*) gives (*c*), a protonated form of humulene which, by further cyclization and Wagner-Meerwein rearrangement, affords the plant sesquiterpene longifolene. Superficially this product contains three isoprene units irregularly linked, but the tracer experiments were consistent only with the rearrangement route indicated. Yet another variant cyclization yields (*d*), from which pyrethrosin and similar sesquiterpenes can be derived, and thence (*e*), parent of the cadinene type. Reactions parallel to those in the longifolene sequence, followed by a ring-opening, explain the non-isoprenoid structure and isotope data for the mould metabolite helminthosporal.

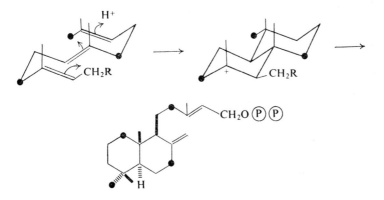

Figure 4.10. *Biogenesis of a bicyclic precursor of diterpenes. The heavy dots mark carbon from* $C_{(2)}$ *of mevalonate; R is the dimethylallyl pyrophosphate group.*

Diterpenes

The cyclic diterpenes presumably arise from geranylgeranyl phosphate, and Ruzicka showed that all the known types could arise following an initial cyclization of the type shown in Figure 4.10; such a cyclization, initiated by protonation, is analogous to the cyclization of squalene, initiated by oxygenation, discussed later, p. 60. The cyclic precursor shown is manoyl pyrophosphate. From its mode of formation with the first three isoprene units folded in "chair-like" conformation, this necessarily has the typical *trans-anti-trans* stereochemistry, and for most, but not all, diterpenes the absolute configuration is that shown in Figure 4.10.

The most interesting isotope studies have been with fungal diterpenoids, which though a somewhat rare class of compound show special interest as well as experimental convenience. The biogenesis of rosenonolactone, a cometabolite of trichothecin, is outlined in Figure 4.11; the precursor from Figure 4.10 is converted to the allylic cation, which cyclizes in the manner shown, with a 1,2-shift of the methyl group. Oxygenation reactions then yield rosenonolactone. The sequence fully explains the stereochemistry of the product, with its unusual *trans-syn-trans* arrangement, and also the isotopic data: in particular, the labelling of the α-methyl group in ring A, and not the β-carboxyl group, by 2-^{14}C-mevalonate. The oxidation of the original *gem*-dimethyl group has important parallels in the triterpene series.

Figure 4.12 outlines part of a more complex series of metabolites, from *Gibberella* sp., including the important hormone gibberellic acid

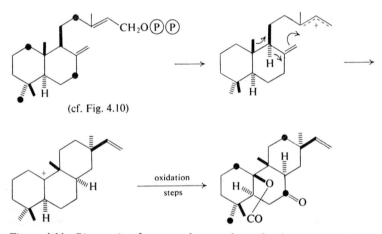

Figure 4.11. *Biogenesis of rosenonolactone from the diterpene precursor, showing labelling from 2-^{14}C-mevalonate.*

which is found in higher plants. Compounds in this series are enantiomeric with the "normal" diterpenes, and the precursor must be the mirror-image of that shown in Figure 4.10. The formation of ring D is known to involve Wagner-Meerwein rearrangement as shown, and not the alternative 1,2-methyl shift; the two routes lead to different labelling in the vinylidene grouping when 1-^{14}C-acetate is used as precursor. Note how the *trans-anti-cis* configuration of the (−)-kaurene arises, and how in this enantiomeric series it is the β-carbon of the *gem*-dimethyl group which is labelled by ^{14}C-mevalonate, and the α-carbon which ultimately undergoes oxidation. Contraction of ring B in forming gibberellic acid clearly follows the oxidative attack which is partly illustrated in kaurenolide; not all the metabolites of this

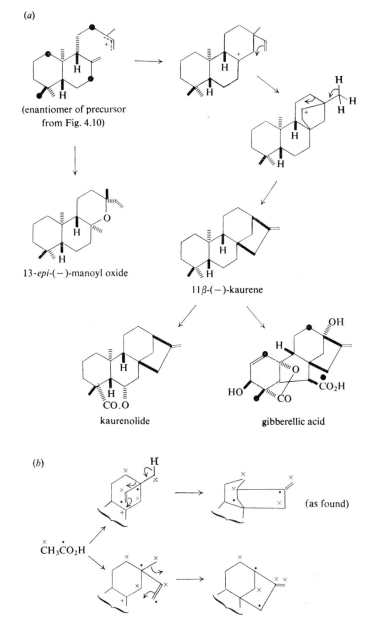

Figure 4.12. (a) *Formation of some metabolites of* Gibberella fujikuroi; (b) *distinction between the route shown in* (a) *and an alternative mechanism, using labelled acetate as precursor.*

series are shown, but the remainder are fully consistent with the sequence given here.

Triterpenes

The hypothesis of concerted cationic cyclizations and rearrangements was first developed in connection with the conversion of squalene, via

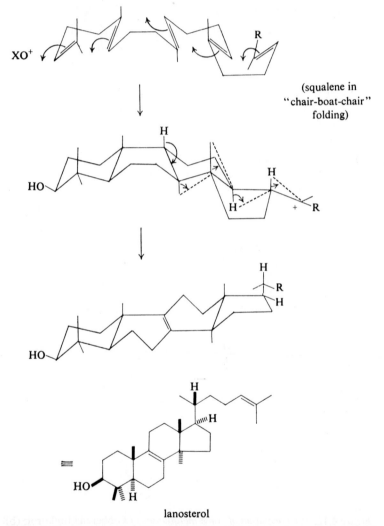

(squalene in "chair-boat-chair" folding)

lanosterol

Figure 4.13. *Oxygenase-catalysed cationic cyclization and rearrangement of squalene to give lanosterol (R = 4-methyl-pent-3-enyl).*

the triterpene lanosterol, into cholesterol. In this case the cationic centre is generated by oxygenation of the squalene, which is the general mechanism in the triterpene series. The oxygen is introduced as an electrophilic agent but derives from gaseous O_2. The precise course of the cyclization and concerted rearrangement reactions which follow is

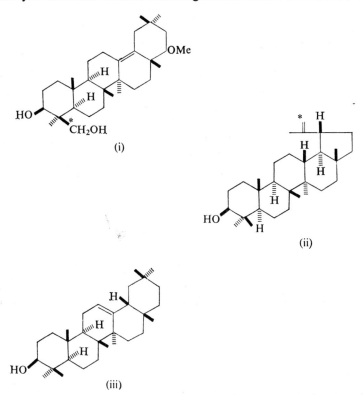

Figure 4.14. *Plant triterpenes soyasapogenol-D (i) and lupeol (ii); in each, the carbon atom marked* (*) *is originally part of a gem-dimethyl group, but when the molecule is labelled by 2-¹⁴C-mevalonate this carbon atom does not acquire labelling. β-Amyrin(iii) is another triterpene, for which direct biosynthesis from all* trans-*squalene has been demonstrated, and occurs widely in plants.*

determined by the conformation in which the flexible all-*trans*-squalene molecule is folded (on the enzyme surface ?). Thus, as shown in Figure 4.13, lanosterol formation requires an initial "chair-boat-chair", or *trans-syn-trans*-perhydrophenanthrene pattern. This mode of cycliz-ation is characteristic of animals* and of the lower plants and micro-

* Steroid synthesis is absent in insects, where the deficiency involves several stages in the isoprenoid sequence, and in bacteria.

organisms; in higher plants, variations lead to other triterpene types, sometimes with more complex rearrangements at the distal end of the molecule, e.g. in forming the pentacyclic soyasapogenol or lupeol types (Figure 4.14). In the case of β-amyrin (Figure 4.14), studies with germinating peas show that this triterpene is formed rather directly from all-*trans*-squalene, as the hypothesis requires. Such considerations provide a full rationalization of structural and stereochemical features; for a fuller account, *see* p. 68.

In the lanosterol/cholesterol sequence the origin of individual carbon atoms, including those involved in the double 1,2-shift of methyl groups, has been fully verified. The enzyme reaction can be carried out *in vitro* and its concerted nature is shown by the failure to exchange protons with added D_2O. The cases of soyasapogenol-D and lupeol (Figure 4.14) are also of interest; these are squalene-derived, and in each of them one carbon from a terminal *gem*-dimethyl group can be distinguished chemically from its neighbour. Stereospecific biogenesis in accordance with the general cyclization mechanism is demonstrated when 2-^{14}C-mevalonate is incorporated.

Carotenoids

Cyclization in the C_{40} series is of limited scope, and is considered along with other reactions on p. 66. This contrast with the behaviour of squalene is probably connected with the more rigid nature of the C_{40} precursor with its central conjugated *trans*-triene system (Figure 4.7).

Modifying Reactions

Lower terpenes

Interconversions of plant terpenes occur extensively, and apparently rapidly, and lead to the numerous variations in unsaturation, oxygenation, etc. found with a single carbon skeleton. Such interconversions are readily rationalized in chemical terms but there is seldom much evidence for their sequence or even their direction. Arguments have been based on frequencies of occurrence, on stereochemical relationships, on interpretations of genetic data, or on changes in composition during plant development, but have not proved definitive. Tracer experiments using "early" precursors (CO_2, mevalonate) have not been sufficiently detailed to reveal later sequences, while the use of "later" precursors raises experimental difficulties. Our knowledge of the basic biosynthetic mechanisms is now sufficient to show which compounds in a series are closest to the open-chain or primary cyclization precursors, but there is scope for considerable experi-

mental study in this field. The extent of some of these further transformations can be illustrated by examples already given—chrysanthemic acid (Figure 4.8), trichothecolone and helminthosporal
(Figure 4.9), the gibberellin series (Figure 4.12).

A somewhat different type of reaction, which probably occurs after
cyclization, is seen in Figure 4.15, summarizing the biogenesis of
plumieride (a plant glycoside) so far as it is understood from tracer
experiments. Here, a terpene, perhaps related to the termite product

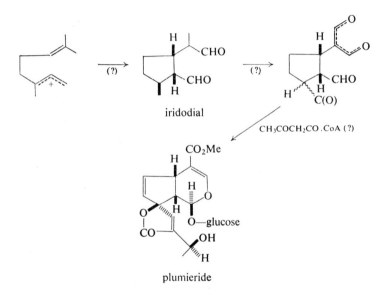

iridodial

CH₃COCH₂CO.CoA (?)

plumieride

*Figure 4.15. Possible sequence in biosynthesis of plumieride from two iso-
prene units and acetoacetate.*

iridodial, reacts with acetoacetate to build up the C_{14} skeleton;
plumieride is not, as might at first seem likely, a degraded sesquiterpene. For iridodial etc., cf. also p. 122.

Triterpenes and steroids

Changes following cyclization have been studied in more detail in the
lanosterol series. In forming cholesterol, three methyl groups are
removed oxidatively as CO_2, probably by way of carboxylic acids; in
addition, the double bond of the side-chain is reduced, and that in the
ring is shifted. The compounds shown in Figure 4.16 have been identified as intermediates but some sequential details remain obscure; for

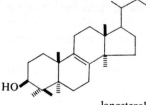

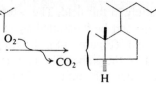

lanosterol   14-*nor*-lanosterol

O_2

other intermediates

$2 CO_2$

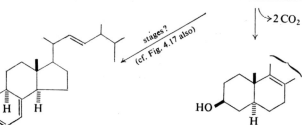

ergosterol   zymosterol

stages?
(cf. Fig. 4.17 also)

O_2 (intermediates?)

cf. Fig. 4.17

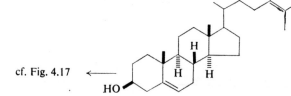

desmosterol

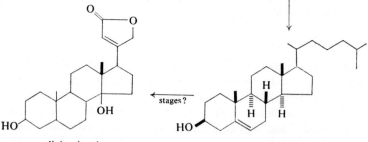

digitoxigenin   stages?   cholesterol

Figure 4.16. Some products formed from lanosterol, including some intermediates in cholesterol formation.

example, the conversion of zymosterol into cholesterol requires oxygen, and might involve an intermediate diene, but ergosterol (*see* below), which has such a diene system, is formed not from zymosterol but from some earlier intermediate.

Cholesterol itself undergoes a wide variety of further transformations in animal metabolism, with which we are not concerned here,

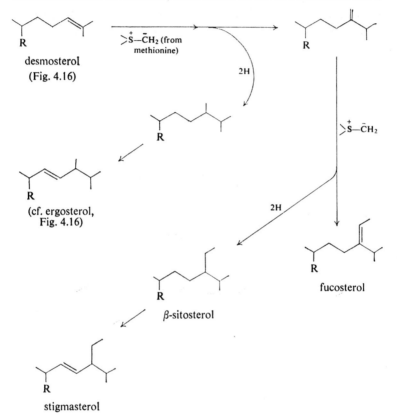

Figure 4.17. *Side-chain addition of methylene groups and related reactions in the β-sitosterol series.*

and also furnishes the carbocyclic portion of the cardiac glycosides (e.g. digitoxigenin, Figure 4.16). Another type of secondary reaction is the addition of extra carbon atoms to the side-chain. This is exemplified in Figure 4.17 for β-sitosterol and related compounds, but is also found in other series, e.g. ergosterol and the fungal triterpenoids. The reaction occurs at the double bond of the side-chain, by transfer from S-adenosylmethionine of a CH_2 group (*not* CH_3), and as shown in the figure this can lead to "extra" methylene, methyl, ethylidene, or ethyl groups. The reaction is presumably a kind of carbene or ylide addition to this rather unreactive double bond; compare the alkylation of ethenoid fatty acids, p. 18.

Carotenoids

The very numerous natural carotenoids differ in the extent of unsaturation, cyclization, and oxygenation reactions of the basic C_{40} skeleton.

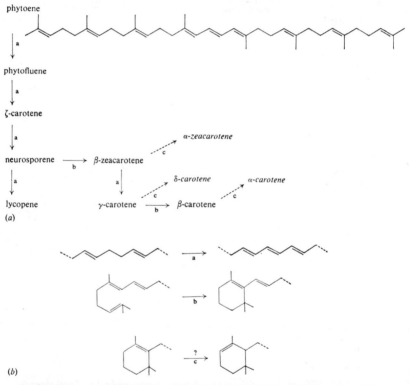

Figure 4.18. (a) *Relationships between some carotenoid hydrocarbons; the origin of the "α-ionone"-type carotenoids (italics) is still uncertain. The designated reactions are as shown in (b).*

The general direction of these processes is fairly clear, but the precise relationships of individual compounds is often conjectural. In the acyclic series, which are the main carotenoids of photosynthetic bacteria, it is known that the parent compound phytoene, $C_{40}H_{64}$ (three conjugated double bonds), undergoes successive dehydrogenation steps at alternate ends of the conjugated chain; four such steps give lycopene, $C_{40}H_{56}$, with eleven conjugated double bonds. For the mono- and bi-cyclic carotenoids of higher plants, in which the rings may be of the α- or β-type, there are similar dehydrogenation series; unfortunately, the substrates of the cyclization steps are not strictly identified, so the relation between the series is uncertain. One possible scheme is shown in Figure 4.18; note that only three reactions suffice to produce fifteen hydrocarbons.

Oxygenation reactions introduce further complications of the same general nature. Illustrative examples are the xanthophylls of the β-carotene series shown in Figure 4.19, and a series of neurosporene

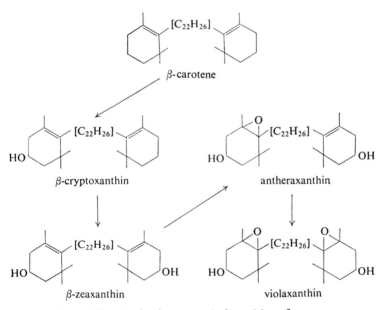

Figure 4.19. Oxidized carotenoids derived from β-carotene.

derivatives from bacteria, Figure 4.20. In all such series the specificity of the enzymes mediating each step is unknown, but parallel reactions of different substrates are very frequently observed, suggesting that the enzymes are relatively non-specific. As discussed in Chapter Six (p. 82) and elsewhere, situations of this kind complicate the interpretation of such experimental data as are available.

Compartmentalization effects in plants

Studies of isoprenoid biosynthesis in intact plants have revealed some interesting anomalies due to the localization of different biosynthetic pathways in different parts of the plant cells. The chloroplasts, site of photosynthetic CO_2 fixation, contain carotenoids and a range of compounds with isoprenoid side-chains—chlorophyll, plastoquinone, vitamin K, tocopherols. Development of the chloroplasts requires light, and under these conditions [14]CO_2 is efficiently incorporated into the chloroplast isoprenoids, but added ^{14}C-mevalonate cannot reach

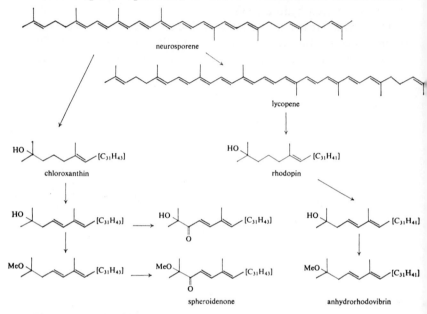

Figure 4.20. *Parallel transformations in xanthophylls of* Rhodospirillum rubrum.

this synthetic site and is not incorporated. Typical cytoplasmic tri-terpenes simultaneously incorporate ^{14}C from mevalonate but not from CO_2. The existence of such effects illustrates the possible complexity of biosynthetic experiments in higher organisms and the dangers involved in their interpretation. On the other hand, moulds and non-photosynthesizing plant tissues such as the tomato fruit utilize mevalonate quite effectively for carotenoid synthesis, and the cell extracts will also utilize isopentenyl and farnesyl pyrophosphates.

FURTHER READING

General

J. H. Richards and J. B. Hendrickson, *The Biosynthesis of Steroids, Terpenes, and Acetogenins*. Benjamin, New York, 1964.

L. Ruzicka, *Experientia*, **9**, 357–367 (1953); *idem, Proc. chem. Soc.*, **1959**, 341–360 (the biogenetic isoprene rule and its history).

G. E. W. Wolstenholme and M. O'Connor (ed.) *CIBA Symposium on the Biosynthesis of Terpenes and Sterols*. Churchill, London, 1959.

See also the references cited for Chapter Five, p. 76.

Special Aspects

G. Popják and J. W. Cornforth, *Advances in Enzymology*, **22**, 281–335 (1960) (cholesterol).

A. F. Wagner and K. Folkers, ibid., **23**, 471–483 (1961) (mevalonic acid).

T. W. Goodwin, ibid., **21**, 295–361 (1959); *idem, The Biosynthesis of Vitamins*. Academic, New York, 1963 (carotenoids).

S. L. Jensen, G. Cohen-Bazire and R. Y. Stanier, *Nature*, **192**, 1167 (1961) (a carotenoid "grid").

J. G. Kisser, in W. Ruhland (ed.) *Handbuch der Pflanzenphysiologie. X. Der Stoffwechsel sekundärer Pflanzenstoffe*. Springer, Berlin, 1958, pp. 91–131 (physiological aspects).

A. J. Haagen-Smit, ibid. pp. 52–90; *idem*, in E. Guenther (ed.) *The Essential Oils*, Vol. I, van Nostrand, New York, 1948, pp. 15–84 (physiological aspects).

CHAPTER FIVE

Biosynthesis in Cell-free Systems

Most of the biosynthetic processes dealt with in this book have been studied by methods which are more or less indirect. Only in a few cases have the reacting systems been found available for study by the more typical methods of biochemistry which normally involve some degree of isolation of the experimental material from other cell activities. Usually, such isolation is achieved physically, by killing and fragmenting the cells and, whenever possible, by further fractionation of the cell debris; such methods have been the standard procedure in biochemical studies of primary metabolic processes, but so far they have found only limited application in the study of secondary biosynthetic systems. The reasons for this are not readily apparent, but it is possible that these systems require integrated associations of enzymes, perhaps connected with structural elements in the intact cell, which are particularly sensitive to disruption. Certainly, procedures designed to give cell-free preparations active in secondary biosynthetic processes have often proved difficult and unreliable, though there seems to be no *a priori* reason why they should not become more accessible as techniques improve and as more interest is devoted to this aspect of the subject by experienced enzymologists. Meanwhile, most of our knowledge of secondary biosynthesis comes from studies with intact cells or whole organisms, and it is partly because such methods form a less widely-recognized tool in biochemistry that some space in this book has been devoted to their consideration in general terms.

However, there are some instances where the "direct" biochemical methods have been successfully applied, and with improved procedures we would expect such cases to be multiplied, so that some special reference to this kind of approach is also desirable. Fortunately, it can be illustrated by some exceedingly elegant studies on a biosynthetic sequence of major importance, namely, that from mevalonic acid to squalene as outlined in Chapter Four. We shall not be concerned with details of experimental procedure such as may be found in original papers, nor with presenting all the evidence for every step in the sequence. Instead, by considering the work of two different groups, some illustrations of methods of approach, and sequences of reasoning, will be attempted.

Isopentenyl pyrophosphate

Collaborators in the Munich laboratories of Professor Lynen made an extended study of squalene biosynthesis using cell-free extracts obtained from bakers' yeast by a variety of disruptive methods. The complete system effected squalene synthesis, provided that both ATP and the reduced coenzyme, TPNH, were available, from either mevalonic acid or 5-phosphomevalonate, the latter being independently known as the first product formed from mevalonate. The problem was to resolve this obviously complex sequence into simpler stages and, ultimately, into discrete enzymic reaction steps. Extensive use was made of isotopically-labelled substrates, not primarily to ascertain the patterns of isotope incorporation but for the extra facility these afford in detecting reactions proceeding on a small scale.

In the absence of ATP, both mevalonate and 5-phosphomevalonate remained unchanged, but the requirement for TPNH provided an initial resolution of the system, since in its absence a different product was obtained. This contained both ^{32}P and ^{14}C when 5-^{32}P-phospho-2-^{14}C-mevalonate was used, and was probably a true intermediate, since, when added to the complete enzyme system with TPNH (and without ATP), ^{14}C-squalene was produced. The ^{32}P of this product was split off with a readiness which suggested the presence of an allylic phosphate, while enzymic hydrolysis with a phosphatase gave ^{32}P-pyrophosphate. The organic moiety was identified as the C_{15} alcohol farnesol by chromatography of the ^{14}C-labelled material, and was confirmed by conversion into crystalline derivatives; the distribution of the ^{14}C was outlined by ozonolysis. The intermediate accumulating in the absence of TPNH was thus identified as farnesyl pyrophosphate, and at this stage the overall sequence could be formulated as:

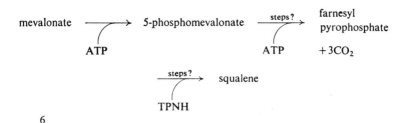

Squalene synthesis in the complete system, also farnesyl pyrophosphate synthesis in the absence of TPNH, were alike inhibited by iodoacetamide, an inhibitor of enzymes which depend upon sulphydryl groups for their activity. This allowed a further resolution, since with iodoacetamide inhibition a new intermediate accumulated and could be detected by electrophoretic separation. The new intermediate incorporated both ^{32}P and ^{14}C from $5\text{-}^{32}P$-phospho-$2\text{-}^{14}C$-mevalonate, but ^{14}C supplied as $1\text{-}^{14}C$-mevalonate was released as CO_2 and not incorporated into the new intermediate, which therefore contained only 5 of the 6 carbon atoms of mevalonate. As in farnesyl pyrophosphate, a pyrophosphate ester group was detected. Hydrolysis with phosphatase gave an alcohol which was converted by successive enzymic oxidation (using alcohol- and aldehyde-dehydrogenases) into 3-methylbut-3-enoic acid, $CH_2\text{:}CMe\cdot CH_2CO_2H$. By comparison with synthetic materials the alcohol was identified as 3-methylbut-3-enol and the intermediate pyrophosphate as 3-methylbut-3-enyl pyrophosphate ("isopentenyl" pyrophosphate). It accumulates when the enzyme catalysing its isomerization to dimethylallyl pyrophosphate is inhibited by iodoacetamide. Synthetic isopentenyl pyrophosphate, labelled with ^{14}C, was converted enzymically into farnesyl pyrophosphate and squalene, also into cholesterol by a liver preparation, and was thus identified as the biologically active "isoprene unit".

The stages between isopentenyl and farnesyl pyrophosphates could at this stage be predicted, and we shall not consider their detailed elucidation. However, the formation of isopentenyl phosphate itself is of some interest. At this stage the reaction could be summarized:

By chromatographic fractionation of the enzymes in a yeast autolysate, a preparation catalysing only a partial conversion of 5-phosphomevalonate was obtained, allowing the formulation:

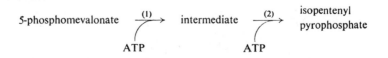

Using the enzyme fraction catalysing only step (1), the intermediate was shown to be mevalonic acid 5-pyrophosphate, and its formation was formulated as

$$\text{5-phosphomevalonate} \xrightarrow{(1)} \text{mevalonic 5-pyrophosphate}$$
$$+\text{ATP} \qquad\qquad\qquad +\text{ADP}$$

The evidence adduced for this formulation can be summarized as follows. The ADP formed was measured by coupling the system with the DPNH reduction of phosphoenol pyruvate, and was shown to be equivalent to the amount of mevalonate used. The intermediate contained one phosphate group labile to acid hydrolysis and two phosphate groups labile to phosphatase, and was thus a pyrophosphate, while the organic moiety was shown to be mevalonic acid and was converted into 5-phosphomevalonate, squalene, etc., in suitable enzyme systems. The intermediate was prepared labelled with ^{14}C at $C_{(2)}$ and converted into ^{14}C-squalene, also with ^{14}C at $C_{(1)}$; using the latter, it was confirmed that reaction (2), in which $^{14}CO_2$ was split off, also required ATP.

Although the foregoing does not cover the complete elucidation of this section of the sequence, nor indeed does it cover more than a small part of the contributions of the Munich school, it aptly illustrates the approach utilized. Note, in particular, the initial use of cofactor requirements or inhibitor effects on the whole multi-enzyme system, obtaining major resolutions of the successive steps, and subsequent refinement by the more arduous method of fractionation of the actual enzymes.

Squalene synthesis

Although the initial steps in the mevalonate-squalene sequence are of the most general importance in isoprenoid biogenesis, the final steps leading to the formation of squalene itself also raise interesting problems, which have been very elegantly resolved by J. W. Cornforth, G. Popják, and their co-workers, who used an enzyme preparation from rat-liver microsomes. Their work illustrates a somewhat different type of approach, essentially that of the organic chemist, with particular utilization of double isotope labelling and, in place of tracer labelling with radioactive isotopes, the use of heavy isotopes at high levels. Heavy-isotope work of this kind requires quite different methods for the final examination of the labelled molecules, and the data obtained, especially when deuterium is used, can be misleading unless expertly handled.

The overall conversion of farnesyl pyrophosphate into squalene involves reduction (for which TPNH is specifically required) and dimerization, and can be written:

$$
\left.
\begin{array}{l}
R . CMe{=}CH . CH_2O \; \textcircled{P} \; \textcircled{P} \\[1em]
R . CMe{=}CH . CH_2O \; \textcircled{P} \; \textcircled{P}
\end{array}
\right\}
\xrightarrow{\;2H\;}
\quad
\begin{array}{l}
R . CMe{=}CH{-}CH_2 \\
\qquad\qquad\quad | \\
R . CMe{=}CH{-}CH_2
\end{array}
$$

The mechanism of this reductive dimerization was by no means obvious, the essential problem concerning the fates of hydrogen atoms in the reagents and their origins in the product, in particular in the central —$CH_2 \cdot CH_2$— group. Earlier work on the overall synthesis from mevalonate seemed to show that two hydrogen atoms of the squalene were contributed by water protons, but when a more careful study was made, using farnesyl pyrophosphate, the immediate squalene precursor, these earlier results were found to be misleading. In tritiated water there was no significant incorporation of radioactivity into the squalene, but when tritiated TPNH was used tritium incorporation occurred, to the extent of approximately *one* atom of TPNH hydrogen per molecule of squalene. Further confirmation of this somewhat surprising result came from experiments with a doubly-labelled substrate, synthetic 1-T-2-^{14}C-farnesyl pyrophosphate. From the changed tritium/^{14}C ratio in squalene formed from this, only three of the four labelled hydrogen atoms had been incorporated. Absolute proof was provided by the use, first of synthetic 5,5-D_2-2-^{14}C-mevalonate (*i.e.* with two deuterium atoms at $C_{(5)}$), second of 1,1-D_2-2-^{14}C-farnesyl pyrophosphate. In each case the central pair of carbon atoms in the squalene formed carried only three of the original four deuterium atoms. In these experiments the ^{14}C content was used to calculate percentage conversions and as a criterion of purification. The squalene was purified via the thiourea clathrate and subjected to ozonolysis on a small scale (*ca.* 10 mg). About 2 mg of purified succinic acid was obtained, mostly but not entirely derived from the central carbon atoms; the ^{14}C data provided the necessary correcting factors. Mass spectroscopic examination now showed conclusively that the central fragment carried three deuterium atoms, i.e. that the dimerization proceeds thus:

$$
\left.
\begin{array}{l}
R . CMe{=}CH . CD_2 . O \; \textcircled{P} . \textcircled{P} \\[1em]
R . CMe{=}CH . CD_2 . O \; \textcircled{P} . \textcircled{P}
\end{array}
\right\}
\xrightarrow{\;2H\;}
\quad
\begin{array}{l}
R . CMe{=}CH . CHD \\
\qquad\qquad\qquad | \\
R . CMe{=}CH . CD_2
\end{array}
$$

The lack of any isotope effect in all these results, despite the considerable differences in reactivity between hydrogen, deuterium and tritium, showed that the reaction sequence in which the fourth hydrogen is displaced must be highly stereospecific, whatever its mechanism, while the asymmetrical labelling of the squalene showed that this redistribution of hydrogen occurred at a stage subsequent to farnesyl pyrophosphate rather than by any kind of exchange mechanism.

With some choice of intimate mechanism, it now seems clear that the coupling of farnesyl pyrophosphate proceeds, as shown in Figure 4.6, after rearrangement of one molecule to nerolidyl pyrophosphate. The two then couple with phosphate elimination, to give a product of the type

$$R.CMe.CH{=}CD.CD_2CH{=}CMe.R$$
$$\underset{O\,\textcircled{P}\,\textcircled{P}}{|}$$

This contains the three residual hydrogen atoms required by the data (shown above as deuterium) and is now subjected to hydride reduction, by TPNH, with allylic displacement of the pyrophosphate. The stereospecificity of this final step was also elucidated, with regard to both the TPNH and the squalene. Using tritium as label, it was shown that only one of the two available hydrogen atoms of TPNH was transferred: specifically, the "β" hydrogen which is also utilized by glucose-6 phosphate dehydrogenase. Using fully deuterated TPNH for the reduction, and isolating mono-deuterosuccinic acid from the central portion of the squalene, this was shown to be dextrorotatory, with the absolute configuration $(+)$-2(S)-2-deuterosuccinic acid. This established the configuration of the squalene correspondingly as

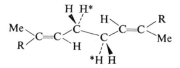

where the hydrogen transferred from TPNH is one of those marked (*).

As already mentioned, this work was executed using an enzyme preparation from rat-liver microsomes. Although certain of the data could, perhaps, have been obtained by studying squalene synthesis in intact cells, the conclusive nature of the results described would have been very difficult to match. For example, it would be quite impracticable in whole cells to label selectively with tritium the TPNH used in the dimerization step, without simultaneously labelling, say, the

TPNH used in mevalonate synthesis. Complete but selective deuteration of the TPNH would be equally impossible, while it is doubtful whether substrates such as farnesyl pyrophosphate would enter the cells at all. Similar objections likewise apply to many hypothetical experiments which might have elucidated other transformations in comparable detail; so long as biosynthetic studies must be carried out by manipulations of intact cells, many aspects of the subject must remain, literally, inaccessible.

FURTHER READING

The experiments summarized in this chapter are fully described in the following papers:

F. Lynen, H. Eggerer, U. Henning and I. Kessel, *Angewandte Chemie*, **70**, 738 (1958).

U. Henning, E. M. Moslein and F. Lynen, *Arch. Biochem. Biophys.*, **83**, 259 (1959).

G. Popják, D. S. Goodman, J. W. Cornforth, R. H. Cornforth and R. Ryhage, *J. Biol. Chem.*, **236**, 1934 (1961); **237**, 56 (1962).

J. W. Cornforth, R. H. Cornforth, C. Donninger, G. Popják, G. Ryback and G. J. Schroepfer, *Biochem. Biophys. Res. Comm.*, **11**, 129 (1963).

CHAPTER SIX

Shikimic Metabolites

Higher plants contain a very large number and variety of compounds which are biosynthetically related to the aromatic amino-acids and derive from the "shikimic acid pathway". In this respect they differ markedly from the fungi etc., in which such metabolites—though by no means rare—are relatively unimportant. As shown in Figure 6.1, the shikimic acid pathway uses phosphoenol-pyruvate and erythrose-4 phosphate; thus, it is closely connected with pathways of sugar metabolism which are particularly important in photosynthesizing organisms (*see* Chapter One), and this may explain the special prominence of shikimic metabolites in higher plants. The shikimic pathway is outlined in Figure 6.1, and the methods employed for its elucidation are discussed in Chapter Seven. Phenylalanine and tyrosine are the most important products of the pathway (and regulate its initial step by specific feedback controls), but the branching pathway to anthranilic acid thence to tryptophane) is also of primary importance.

In addition to alkaloids and other nitrogenous products discussed in Chapter Eight, secondary metabolites are derived from the pathway at several stages, notably (*a*) quinic acid, which accumulates free or in combined forms and is produced from 5-dehydroquinic acid, (*b*), protocatechuic and gallic acids, and their derivatives, which derive from 5-dehydroshikimic acid, (*c*) a range of hydroxybenzoic acids and derivatives, which may derive from chorismic acid, and (*d*) cinnamic acid derivatives, the "C_6C_3" metabolites, formed from phenylalanine and tyrosine, which are the most important examples.

Simple C_6C_3 Derivatives

An enzyme converting phenylalanine into cinnamic acid directly is widely distributed in plants; in a narrower range of species (mostly grasses), the analogous deamination of tyrosine to *p*-coumaric acid also occurs, but, in general, phenylalanine is the key substrate. Figure 6.2 shows the most common sequence of hydroxylation and methylation products then formed, the *ortho*-oxygenation pattern

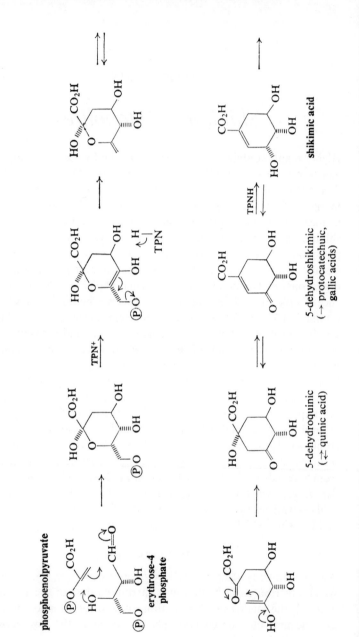

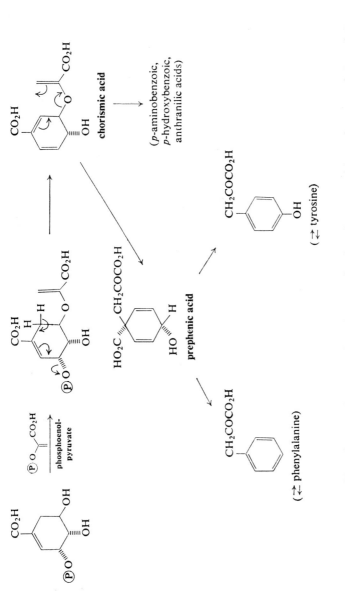

Figure 6.1. The "Shikimic Acid" pathway with suggested mechanisms for three key steps: (a) combination of C_3 and C_4 units from sugar metabolism; (b) cyclization; (c) insertion of second C_3 unit.

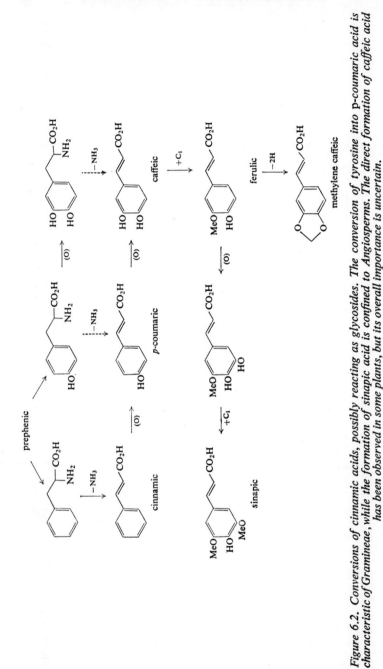

Figure 6.2. Conversions of cinnamic acids, possibly reacting as glycosides. The conversion of tyrosine into p-coumaric acid is characteristic of Gramineae, while the formation of sinapic acid is confined to Angiosperms. The direct formation of caffeic acid has been observed in some plants, but its overall importance is uncertain.

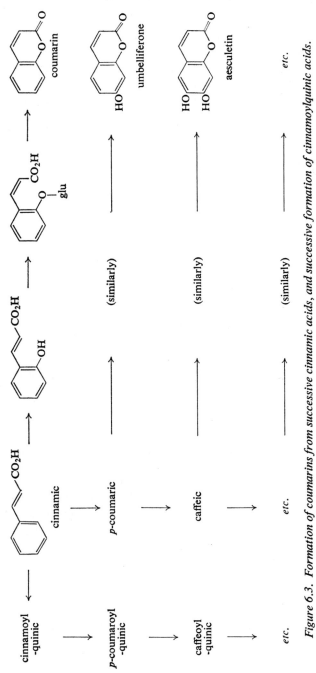

Figure 6.3. *Formation of coumarins from successive cinnamic acids, and successive formation of cinnamoylquinic acids.*

being, in fact, as characteristic of shikimic derivatives as the *meta*-oxygenation of polyketides. The fate of the cinnamic acids thus formed is complex and varies considerably from one plant group to another. A substantial part of the *p*-coumaric acid is used for flavonoid synthesis (p. 86), and in woody plants a large proportion of the cinnamic acids is eventually incorporated into lignin. With certain exceptions, free phenols do not normally accumulate save in "dead" tissues such as heartwood; thus, the cinnamic acids of Figure 6.2 occur mainly as simple conjugation products—esters with methanol, quinic acid, or glucose, or phenol glycosides—or in chemically modified forms. In the latter case it is seldom clear whether a "set" of compounds corresponding to the acids of Figure 6.2 arises by parallel transformations

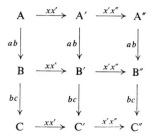

Figure 6.4. A simple "metabolic grid" in which parallel reactions represent analogous transformations catalysed, in this example by enzymes of only relative specificity. E.G. enzyme bc transforms B, B′ and B″ but at different rates; enzyme xx′ similarly transforms A, B and C. There are, thus, six distinct routes from A to C″, some of which will be more important than others, i.e. solutions of the situation are of a quantitative kind.

of the individual acids, or by conversion of a single acid followed by reactions analogous to those in Figure 6.2. For example, in lignins, the hydroxylation pattern is usually comparable to that in cinnamic acids from the same source and, probably, the different cinnamic acids are incorporated by parallel reactions. On the other hand, in flavonoids the hydroxylation pattern is established separately by reactions occurring within the flavonoid series.

As a further complication, it may be uncertain whether the cinnamic acids react as such or in the form of glycosides or similar conjugates. Thus, as shown in Figure 6.3, a series of coumarins is formed from successive cinnamic acids, with glucosides as intermediates. On the other hand, there is a series of cinnamoyl-quinic acids in which, it is believed, hydroxylation of the combined forms is successive.

Situations of this kind arise frequently in series of natural products, and can be described formally in terms of a "metabolic grid" (Figure 6.4). Such grids, not necessarily two-dimensional, are exemplified in polyketide phenols, in carotenoids, in flavonoids, and possibly in alkaloid series, and pose difficult problems. The grid represents intersecting sets of parallel transformations, and the existence of the compounds thus related implies that at least one set of enzymic reactions occurs analogously with different substrates. If we admit that all the enzymes have specificities of this kind, i.e. relative (quantitative) rather than absolute (qualitative), we see that there are not necessarily any unique routes to particular compounds, but that the importance of alternative routes is to be estimated quantitatively. The exact solution of such situations is largely beyond the reach of present experimental methods, but recognition of their nature avoids many apparent contradictions.

Lignins and related compounds

In woody plants, held to be phylogenetically primitive, a high proportion of the pool of free or combined cinnamic acids is transformed, as cells "die", into lignins; these are polymers based on the cinnamyl alcohols. The polymerization is oxidative, comparable to the coupling reactions discussed in Chapter Two, and leads to C—C and C—O linkages involving both the aromatic rings and the side-chains. Apparently, the polymerization is random, involving any of the available substrates; it is further complicated by secondary reactions such as esterification, further oxidation, *etc.*, and it occurs within a matrix of cellular polysaccharides *etc.* which may also be involved, so that the final "lignin structure" is a matter of statistical definition. Several biosynthetic studies indicate that the monomer units are the cinnamic acids derived as in Figure 6.2, with tyrosine as an exceptional precursor, and with sinapic acid peculiar to angiosperms. Studies with Coniferae suggest that reduction follows, and the cinnamyl alcohols then accumulate as glycosides—principally as coniferin, coniferyl β-D-glucoside. At a suitable stage of cell development the glycosides are hydrolysed and the alcohols then subjected to oxidative polymerization. The role of the intermediate glycosides is very similar to that in coumarin formation (Figure 6.3).

Other simple derivatives of the cinnamyl alcohols (Figure 6.5) are the common allylbenzenes, which arise by reduction of the alcohols with double-bond migration. The oligomeric lignans and similar heartwood constituents are biosynthetic relatives of lignin, illustrating some of the ways in which cinnamyl alcohols may be oxidatively

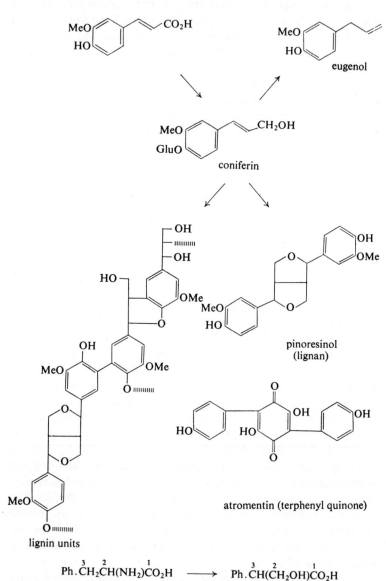

Figure 6.5. Further C_6C_3 derivatives. The "lignin" structure is only a partial representation of typical units in the polymer; lignans also show a greater variety of linkages. Tropic acid shows a unique rearrangement of the C_6C_3 chain.

coupled. A rather different combination of two C_6C_3 units is seen in the terphenylquinones that occur in several of the higher fungi. Such fungi may also contain lignin-like phenolic polymers, which frequently contain units of C_6C_3 type. Sometimes the monomer phenols are synthesized by the fungus via shikimic acid, but sometimes they are obtained parasitically from the host plant, e.g. by the breakdown of lignins or from lignin precursors.

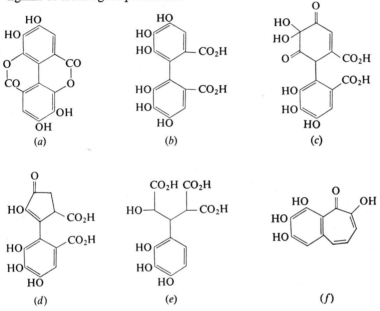

Figure 6.6. Coupling products from gallic acid. Ellagic acid (a) *is the "free" form of the coupled acid* (b); *the acids* (b-e) *occur in the hydrolysable tannins as esters with polygalloyl-glucose. Purpurogallin* (f) *is an alternative oxidation product from the acid* (b).

Tropic acid (an esterifying acid in the tropane alkaloid series) represents an anomalous C_6C_3 product; tracer experiments show that it contains the carbon skeleton of phenylalanine, but with the carboxyl group $C_{(1)}$ transferred from $C_{(2)}$ to $C_{(3)}$. Nothing is known about the mechanism of this remarkable rearrangement, but a possible inter-molecular mechanism would be by formation of a terphenyl derivative (or a suitable lignan), followed by fission of the dimeric intermediate.

C_6C_1 and C_6C_2 Compounds

A variety of simple hydroxybenzoic acids and derivatives occurs in plants. Some of these correspond to the hydroxycinnamic acids (p-hydroxybenzoic, vanillic, syringic; cf. Figure 6.2), have a similar taxonomic distribution, and are probably formed from the C_6C_3 series. This is also true for the C_6C_1 and C_6C_2 precursor units in certain alkaloids (Chapter Eight, p. 112). Similarly, 3,4-dihydroxyaceto-phenone, which occurs as the 3-β-D-glucoside in spruce, is formed from phenylalanine via caffeic acid, with loss of $C_{(1)}$; compare the alkaloid ephedrine, p. 111. Other acids, notably salicylic, protocatechuic, and gallic acids, arise from earlier steps in the shikimic pathway, as noted in Figure 6.1; they occur both free and in various combinations. Derivatives of gallic acid are the most important (Figure 6.6). "Hydrolysable tannins" are based on galloyl- and galloyl-depside-esters of glucose, quinic acid, etc. (gallotannins); in some (ellagitan-nins), the combined gallic acid has undergone oxidative coupling and further transformations. These ellagic acid derivatives are mainly characteristic of woody dicotyledons.

$C_6C_3(C_2)_n$ Compounds

In a very wide range of compounds, cinnamic acids are used as starter units for the addition of short polyketide chains (see Chapter Two). The most important products of these types are the flavonoids, 2-aryl-chroman derivatives, which are further divided into several groups, but Figures 6.7 and 6.8 show a number of related structural types. With a few exceptions, all these compounds are products from higher plants, in which they sometimes occur free but, more commonly, are combined as glycosides. As colouring matters in flowers and other plant parts these compounds have attracted more botanical attention than most plant metabolites. Others have important actions on animal meta-bolism, like the insecticidal rotenoids or the oestrogenic coumarins. Catechins (flavan-3-ols) and flavan-3,4-diols ("leucoanthocyanidins") form dimers and polymeric products by oxidative coupling, which are important as "condensed tannins" (and as flavour components, e.g. in tea).

Knowledge of the biosynthesis of these compounds is based (a) on structure-comparisons, (b) on precursor-incorporation studies, and (c) on genetic analysis of inheritable chemical differences. Structure analysis indicates the basic relationship of these compounds (see Figures 6.7 and 6.8) and the oxygenation patterns of the two benzene rings usually show quite clearly that one is of polyketide origin and the other of the same type as the natural cinnamic acid derivatives. The variant structures shown in Figure 6.8 substantiate this analysis,

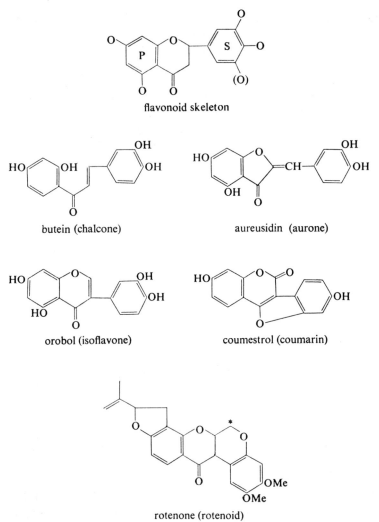

butein (chalcone)   aureusidin (aurone)

orobol (isoflavone)   coumestrol (coumarin)

rotenone (rotenoid)

Figure 6.7. The basic skeleton of flavonoids (ring P, polyketide; ring S, from shikimic) and some related compounds. Some chalcones are intermediates in flavonoid synthesis, and aurones are alternative products. In isoflavones and 3-phenyl-coumarins, the aryl group has migrated to the adjacent carbon, as also in rotenoids; the latter have an isopentenyl residue and an extra carbon atom, marked (*), from the C_1 pool-perhaps originally an —OMe group.

which has been completely confirmed by precursor-incorporation studies.

Thus, for example, in buckwheat (*Fagopyrum*), labelled acetate is

7

incorporated selectively into the phloroglucinol ring of quercetin, but phloroglucinol itself is not incorporated, while shikimic acid and phenylalanine or phenylpyruvic acid are specific precursors of the C_6C_3 portion (Figure 6.9). Though quercetin has the 3′,4′-dihydroxy-phenyl ring, p-coumaric acid is the best C_6C_3 precursor, and caffeic acid is not incorporated: the final hydroxylation pattern of flavonoids is established at a later stage. On the other hand, the hydroxylation pattern of the polyketide ring is established prior to chalcone form-ation, as one would expect. Thus, as shown in Figure 6.9, the tri-

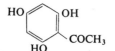

phloracetophenone

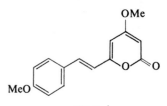

yangonin

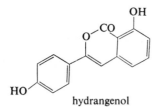

hydrangenol

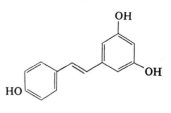

resveratrole

Figure 6.8. Variants on flavonoid biosynthesis. In phloracetophenone, acetate replaces a C_6C_3 unit as "starter", while in yangonin only two C_2 units have been added to the p-coumaryl group. Hydrangenol shows the alternative (aldol-type) cyclization of the polyketide, which by decarboxylation leads to stilbenes.

hydroxychalcone is incorporated into formononetin, but not into biochanin-A (5-hydroxy-formononetin). As shown in Figure 6.9, the p-coumaric and acetate units are combined, presumably as p-cou-maroyl- and acetyl-CoA, to give the chalcone, also found to be a good quercetin precursor. This general scheme has been confirmed with other flavonoids, including isoflavonoids in which the aryl group migrates to an adjacent carbon at a later stage in synthesis.

For reactions subsequent to chalcone formation our evidence is generally less direct. Some comes from genetic studies, the special difficulties of which are discussed in Chapter Seven. However, the combination of data to give a general picture can be attempted

(Figure 6.10). If we regard the "main" sequence as leading from chalcones to anthocyanidins, genetic data suggest that the "branch" pathways to aurones, to flavones, and to flavonols occur in that order. They also imply that distinctive patterns of hydroxylation in the shikimic-derived ring are established between the aurone and flavone

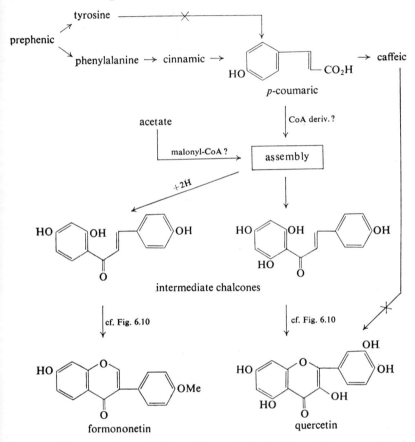

Figure 6.9. Biosynthesis of a flavonol (quercetin) and isoflavone (formononetin) via chalcones, as established by the use of labelled precursors.

branches. Chemotaxonomic evidence (i.e. the analysis of flavonoid content in relation to the classification of plant species) suggests a generic relationship between dihydroflavonols, flavonols, and flavandiols, while the anomalous isoflavonoids and related compounds are of very restricted occurrence. The major natural flavanones, dihydroflavonols, and catechins are all found to have the same

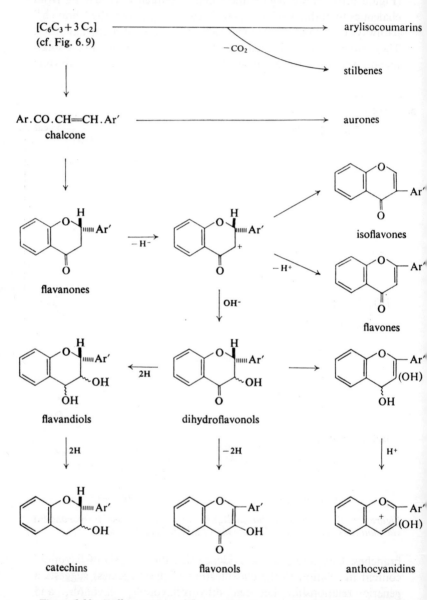

Figure 6.10. Differentiation of flavonoids in the sequence indicated by genetic and other data. Hydroxylation is omitted; the oxygenation pattern of the shikimic-derived ring Ar′ is established at the flavonone stage, and that of the acetate-derived ring Ar is established in polyketide cyclization.

stereochemistry at $C_{(2)}$. Figure 6.10 shows how these relationships are concordant with a plausible chemical sequence to the different flavonoid types.

The key reactions of Figure 6.10 are written, following a suggestion of Birch, as oxidations of flavanones at the enolic position, followed either by hydration (to dihydro-flavonols etc.) or by proton elimination to give flavones. Isoflavone formation then appears as an alternative step to flavone formation, since the two reactions follow sterically different courses (hydrogen quasi-axial for flavones; aryl group quasi-axial for isoflavones). Formation of the flavandiols, catechins, and anthocyanidins then follows rational courses as shown. Not shown in Figure 6.10 are the hydroxylation reactions which lead to characteristic mixtures of 4'-hydroxy-, 3',4'-dihydroxy-, and 3',4',5'-trihydroxyflavonoids, independently of the oxygenation pattern of the C_6C_3 pool; these must operate mainly at the flavanone stage, but not necessarily exclusively. Again, it is uncertain whether the compounds involved in all these transformations are the free phenols, as shown in Figure 6.10, or glycosidic or other derivatives, but it is known (largely from genetic studies) that the final pattern of glycosylation, methylation, etc. is established at a late stage when the flavonoids are fully differentiated, and in a few cases some sequential details are known. Other transformations include alkylation with isopentenyl groups (*see* Chapter Four), oxidative coupling, etc. Once again, the whole set of reactions constitutes a complex example of the "metabolic grid" already discussed, and is to be understood in this manner. Concerning more complex (and less common) flavonoid analogues, much hypothetical detail has been written, but until our knowledge of the main pathways of flavonoid differentiation is more advanced, these exercises have little practical significance. On the other hand, the flavonoids have considerable botanical interest and extensive correlations with genetic and chemotaxonomic studies are possible, so that further experimental work on flavonoid biosynthesis promises to be of fundamental importance.

Further Transformations of Plant Phenolics

One important aspect of the study of plant products is that it is often uncertain whether a particular product is present in the living plant or is the result of post-mortem changes. Such changes can occur spontaneously, or be accelerated as a result of structural damage to the tissues. Enzymes may come into contact with substrates not normally accessible to them, or protecting substances may be decomposed, leaving substrates open to attack. Nearly all the phenolic substances in living plant tissue are combined as glycosides, enzymic hydrolysis of which leads to major post-mortem changes—e.g. the formation of coumarins from *o*-coumaric acid glycosides, already mentioned. Many of the plant samples examined by chemists in the search for new "natural products" have undergone extensive changes of this kind long before they reach the laboratory. Such post-mortem changes may, however, have considerable interest and importance in their own right, since they occur in the harvesting and processing of many plant materials. Many of the examples that have been investigated involve phenolic compounds of the type discussed in this chapter. For example, the non-enzymic discoloration of certain potato varieties is due to autoxidation of chlorogenic (caffeoyl-quinic) acid, catalysed by iron which, in non-colouring varieties, is bound by citric acid. The development of flavour and colour during the processing of tea, coffee, and chocolate is closely connected with complex changes in flavonoid content. These are partly brought about by plant enzymes, partly by micro-organisms, and partly by non-enzymic reactions.

In woody species, even the living plant contains tissues which are effectively "dead" but derived from cells which were once "live", and the changes in phenolic content which occur during this phase of development are again considerable. The most outstanding example is the conversion of monomeric cinnamyl glycosides into lignins, but many more distinctive wood products must be formed analogously. Heartwood constituents such as lignans and stilbenes are examples, as are the polymeric condensed tannins formed from catechins and flavandiols. Much further work will be needed before these important secondary processes are properly understood. Another field of potential interest and importance concerns products formed in plant tissues infected with micro-organisms, either by the plant in response to the infection, or by metabolism of the plant constituents by the micro-organism. In all these situations the phenolic plant constituents seem to play an important role, partly because of their variety and wide distribution and partly because of the readiness with which they will enter into further reactions.

FURTHER READING

Three excellent compendia of recent date cover in detail the material of this chapter, namely:

J. B. Harborne (ed.) *Biochemistry of Phenolic Compounds*. Academic, London, 1964.

T. Swain (ed.) *Chemical Plant Taxonomy*. Academic, London, 1963.

T. A. Geissman (ed.) *The Chemistry of Flavonoid Compounds.* Pergamon, Oxford, 1962.

The individual authors contributing to these three works comprise most of the effective contributors to the subject.

CHAPTER SEVEN

The Study of Biosynthesis in Mutant Organisms

Study of Primary Synthetic Processes

The Shikimic Pathway

The elucidation of the shikimic acid pathway, largely completed by Davis and co-workers in the period 1954–1960, gives us the classic illustration of the use of mutant micro-organisms in biosynthetic studies, and several full reviews are available (p. 106). For our purposes these studies form a useful preliminary. The pathway is one of primary metabolism and leads to a number of essential cell components which, as we shall see, considerably facilitated its investigation. The fact that products from the pathway are also prime precursors of a great many secondary metabolites gives the studies added interest to us, but this is not really relevant to our main purpose, which is to consider the lines of reasoning involved and their application in a wider field.

When mutants arise spontaneously, or when they are obtained artificially by irradiation or treatment with chemical mutagens, the great majority differ from the parent stock in only a single gene; the usual effect is impaired synthesis of a single enzyme. If the damage is of too fundamental a nature the mutants cannot be made to survive or multiply, but in many cases the genetic defect can be made good by external factors. If the affected enzyme is one which brings about one specific step in the synthesis of some essential cell component, the mutant cells will not grow on what is normally an adequate medium, but they will grow if the essential cell component, or some compound which is still convertible into that component, is supplied externally. Clearly, the mere detection of such nutritional requirements gives clues to the special pathway affected. The mutants can now be isolated and grown on their specially-supplemented medium for further study. As they grow, reactions prior to the step affected in the mutation may still occur, so that intermediates in the pathway, or "shunt" products formed from them, may accumulate and be identified;

94

reactions subsequent to the blocked step may be identifiable from
the range of substances which will satisfy the nutritional requirement.
If mutations affecting different stages in the pathway can be obtained,
more detailed information can be acquired. For obvious reasons,
nutritional requirements for large or non-diffusible molecules are
never encountered (cf. Chapter Three); within these limitations the
method is a powerful one for the investigation of primary metabolic
pathways. Contrary to common impression, the method has very little
to do with the science of genetics, though nutritional mutants are also

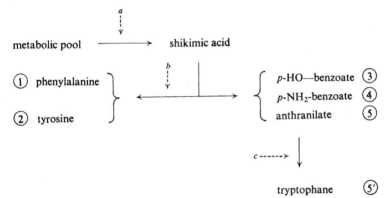

Figure 7.1. Simplified topology of the shikimic acid pathway. Mutations
affecting a step at a cause simultaneous requirements for compounds (1), (2),
(3), (4) and (5) or (5′), alternatively, all met by shikimic acid. Mutants blocked
at b show requirements for (1) and (2) only, which are not met by shikimic acid.
Compounds (5) and (5′) are nutritionally equivalent except in mutants blocked
at c.

very useful in genetic analysis. The primary experimental observation
—growth or non-growth—is easily made, and methods for isolating
nutritional mutants are highly developed. For example, many bacteria
are susceptible to penicillin only during actual growth, a fact which can
be used to destroy most of the non-mutant cells left after mutagenic
treatment, leaving (on the normal medium) the non-growing mutants
for further study on suitably supplemented media.

A key observation for the shikimic acid pathway was that several
mutants of *E. coli* displayed simultaneous requirements for a range of
aromatic amino-acids, all of which could alternatively be met by a
single substance. Specifically, some mutants requiring five amino-
acids (phenylalanine, tyrosine, *p*-aminobenzoate, *p*-hydroxybenzoate,
and tryptophane) would grow equally well if shikimic acid alone were
supplied. Other compounds would replace only some of the amino-

acids required by such mutants, e.g. anthranilic acid in place of trypto-phane. Clearly, the aromatic amino-acids are formed, at least in part, by a common pathway in which shikimic acid or a close derivative is an intermediate. Other mutants showed requirements which could not be met by shikimic acid, and were thus blocked at later stages; sometimes such mutants displayed requirements for a smaller number of sub-stances, e.g. for phenylalanine and tyrosine only. In this manner the general topology of the pathway could be defined, as in Figure 7.1;

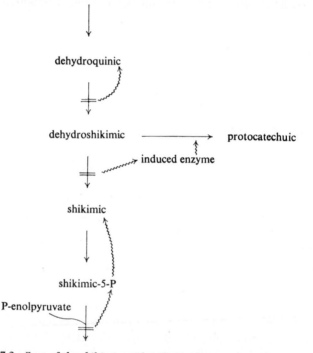

Figure 7.2. Part of the shikimic acid pathway showing, by wavy arrows, the consequences of mutant blocks at different stages.

compare this with the fuller presentation, in (Figure 6.1), which shows the intermediates and discrete enzyme steps so far elucidated by a con-tinuation of the work.

Substances accumulating during the growth of nutritional mutants provided further information. As shown in Figure 7.2, the nature of such accumulations may vary; blocking a particular reaction may lead to accumulation of the immediate substrate of the blocked reaction, or of an earlier intermediate in equilibrium with it, or of a "shunt metabolite" formed from the substrate. The shunt metabolite may be formed either by a normal reaction or by a newly-induced enzyme. All these situations have been found in mutants with defects in the shikimic acid pathway. An *E. coli* mutant, blocked in the conversion of dehydro-quinic to dehydroshikimic acid, accumulates dehydroquinic; another mutant, blocked in the combination of 5-phosphoshikimic with phosphoenolpyruvate, accumulates some 5-phosphoshikimic but mainly shikimic acid. In a *Neurospora* mutant blocked in the conversion of dehydroshikimic to shikimic acid, an initial accumulation of dehydroshikimic induces formation of a new enzyme, which converts it into protocatechuic acid. Conclusions from the nature of accumulation products must therefore be drawn with considerable care.

From this stage onwards, further refinement of hypotheses requires the concerted use of every kind of evidence. Labelling patterns from suitable precursors can be studied in the final products of the pathway and in the compounds accumulated by defective mutants; chemical plausibilities must be adhered to. Ultimately, individual enzymic steps can be studied in cell-free preparations. The blocked mutants remain very useful in these later stages of investigation since they may contain certain of the remaining enzymes in higher-than-normal concentrations, and produce their accumulation products in high yields. In the shikimic acid pathway, the full range of such methods has been applied, though some details still remain uncertain. The interested reader is referred to p. 106 for full accounts in which the complementary applications of these methods can be studied.

Applications to Secondary Biosynthesis

When we consider the application of the methods just outlined to the elucidation of pathways of secondary biosynthesis, a number of difficulties becomes apparent. The first, which affects the experimental approach seriously, is that the simple "growth/non-growth" criterion, with all its attendant techniques, is no longer applicable. Since secondary metabolites are, *ipso facto*, inessential, mutants defective in their synthesis will normally continue to grow alongside the non-mutant parent stock. Their existence is revealed only by a comparatively tedious process of plating-out and examining colonies descended from every individual survivor of the mutagenic treatment. If we are examining synthesis of a pigmented substance this "screening" may be rather easier than when less direct types of examination are needed, but it is generally true that the selection of mutants blocked in secondary pathways is far more tedious and time-consuming; put in another way, the investigator generally has a more limited series of mutants available for study.

Other difficulties are intrinsic to the nature of secondary biosynthetic reactions. As already indicated in discussing the "metabolic grid" problem, many of these reactions are brought about by enzymes which are less specific than those involved in primary metabolism. Thus, though the axiom "one gene—one enzyme" still holds, the extension "one gene—one reaction" does not. Several parallel reactions of different substrates may be blocked by a single mutation, just as effectively as if the block occurred at an earlier common step (Figure 7.3). Equally, compounds of novel structure formed as a result of mutant blocks may still be substrates for the remaining enzymes of a metabolic grid, so that the products finally accumulating are highly modified and the position of the defective step in the sequence is not

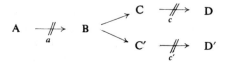

Figure 7.3. Consequences of lack of specificity. In the sequence shown, if the enzymes are wholly specific, a mutant block affecting synthesis of both D and D' must be located at the common step, i.e. at a; blocks at c or c' would affect only D or D' respectively. But if C → D and C' → D' are mediated by a single nonspecific enzyme, the block at c,c' is not readily distinguishable from that at a.

easily deduced. The chemical complexity of the molecules involved can itself lead to additional difficulties by increasing the range of possible transformations.

Tetracyclines

Nevertheless, the method has been usefully applied, and further progress is to be expected. A recent example of its successful use is provided by the work of McCormick and others on the antibiotics of the tetracycline series. They examined a large number of mutants in which antibiotic synthesis was impaired or modified, isolating any novel substances accumulating, and testing possible intermediates for their conversion to tetracyclines. They also applied a "mixed fermentation" method; mutants blocked at different points along a pathway may be able to carry out the complete synthesis when grown together, provided that intact parts of the pathway overlap and (as always) that intermediates can diffuse from one type of cell to the other.

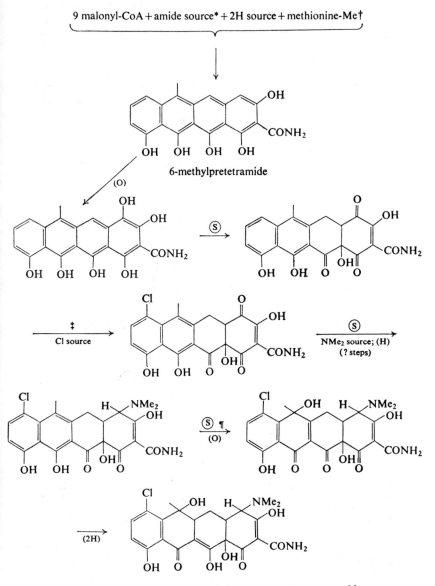

6-methylpretetramide

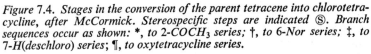

Figure 7.4. Stages in the conversion of the parent tetracene into chlorotetra-cycline, after McCormick. Stereospecific steps are indicated ⓢ. Branch sequences occur as shown: *, to 2-COCH₃ series; †, to 6-Nor series; ‡, to 7-H(deschloro) series; ¶, to oxytetracycline series.

The sequence in tetracycline synthesis is shown in Figure 7.4, and has already been noted from a different viewpoint in Chapter Two. The mutations affecting the earliest steps in the sequence, prior to stabilization of the polyketide assembly, do not cause accumulations of substrates, but lead instead to modified intermediates on which the full sequence of later transformations operates. This is a consequence of the lack of total specificity of the enzymes concerned. Thus, as

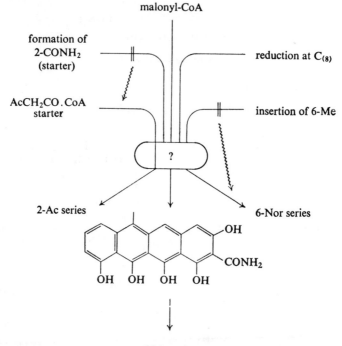

Figure 7.5. Mutant blocks at early stages of tetracycline series, with wavy arrows showing the consequence. Note that for this part of the reaction sequence the mutation effects give no information as to the sequence of steps because of the non-specificity effect analysed in Figure 7.3.

shown in Figure 7.5, mutants in which the carbamido group of the starter unit is not formed use acetoacetyl-CoA as an alternative starter and produce tetracyclines with a 2-acetyl group. Similarly, blocking the C-methylation step leads to the "Nor" series, lacking the 6-methyl group. The reduction step which removes polyketide oxygen at $C_{(8)}$ also occurs prior to polyketide stabilization, and operates in all three series (2-Ac, Nor and 6-Me), but the three steps (starter participation,

C-methylation, reduction) cannot be placed in any sequence from these data—compare Figure 7.3.

Further mutations of strains producing the Nor series can be obtained, and are analogous to mutations affecting parallel steps in the 6-Me series; presumably analogous further mutations could also be obtained in the 2-Ac series. The earliest in the sequence is one of a special type which affects the operation of polyketide stabilization, probably by changing the topography of the matrix. The immediate effect is identical in the 6-Me and Nor series, but the accumulating products differ because of the different structural possibilities of the part-cyclized products (Figure 7.6). When the mutant with matrix defect in the Nor series is grown alongside a fully capable strain in the 6-Me series, only 6-Me products are obtained, which tends to support the idea of a matrix defect; if the partly-cyclized Nor product were a normal intermediate, whose further cyclization in a second step was blocked in the mutant, we should expect the reaction to be completed by the fully capable strain, giving normal products of the Nor series alongside the 6-Me products.

At later stages in the parallel 6-Me and Nor series, further analogous mutant blocks have also been found, although not all the stages of synthesis have been resolved by this method (Figure 7.4). The point of branching in the 6-Me series at which oxytetracycline is formed is shown in Figure 7.4, while the chlorination step, at which two parallel sequences again branch, is also approximately located. Syntheses by mixed cultures of these mutants follow the predicted course, which confirms the sequence given and indicates that the intermediates are diffusible. In pure cultures, several cases of "shunt" transformations of the substrates of blocked steps are observed, and, as before, the course of these transformations is not always parallel. As a single example, Figure 7.7 illustrates consequences of blocking the final reduction step; in the chlorinated 6-Me series the substrate dehydro-compound accumulates, whereas in the non-chlorinated 6-Me series and in the Nor series the dehydro-compounds undergo further trans-formations—which differ in the two series.

Reversion Studies

A somewhat different method, which was usefully applied in studying the biosynthesis of anthraquinones by *Penicillium islandicum*, deserves mention here. Cultures of defective mutants may apparently revert to the parent "wild" type, on repeated subculturing. Whatever the explanation of this phenomenon (and not all microbiologists

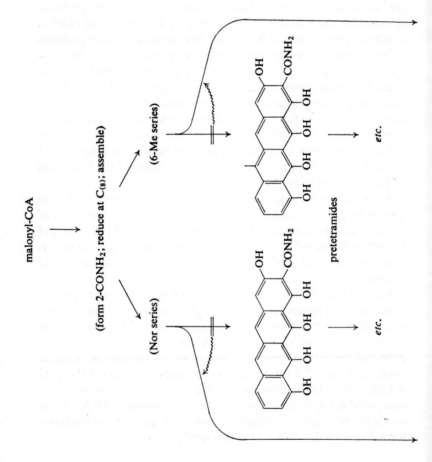

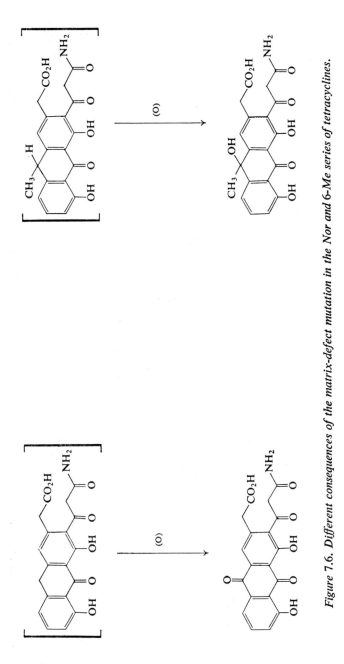

Figure 7.6. Different consequences of the matrix-defect mutation in the Nor and 6-Me series of tetracyclines.

8

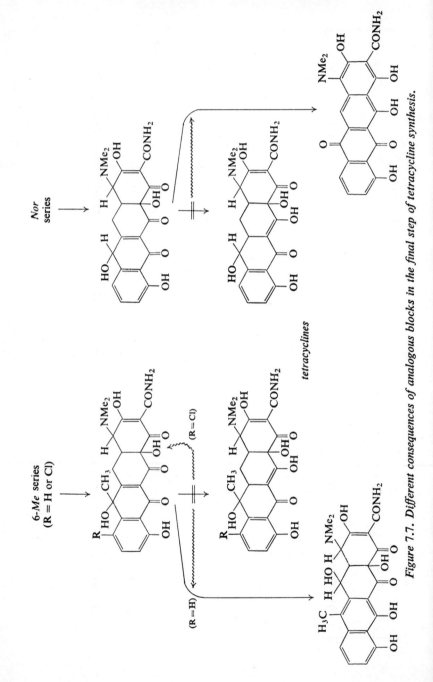

Figure 7.7. Different consequences of analogous blocks in the final step of tetracycline synthesis.

would agree with the orthodox view that it is due to genetic recombination in cultures originally inhomogeneous), it may be accompanied by progressive changes in the pattern of secondary metabolites, which can be interpreted in terms of the systematic restoration of steps in a metabolic sequence (or grid). The data presented in Figure 2.23 are based upon results of this kind.

Plant Genetics and Secondary Metabolism

In studies with higher plants, rational application of the methods just outlined becomes still more difficult. To begin with, the higher plants are multicellular organisms, physiologically specialized in different parts (which all share the same genetic constitution), and with the biochemical activity of each cell regulated indirectly by all the remaining cells. Moreover, all such plants are diploid or polyploid, meaning that the cells contain double or multiple sets of chromosomes, which may carry several combinations of mutant forms of the same gene. Sometimes particular mutant forms may be "dominant" or "recessive" and sometimes their combined effect appears to be simply additive. For numerous reasons, there is no possibility of applying the method of auxotrophic mutants to the study of biosynthesis in plants. On the other hand, the phenomena of inheritance in different mutant lines offer abundant scope for genetic analysis. Unfortunately, though the primary effects of mutations are manifested at the biochemical level, most genetic analysis is based on observations of gross differences in the plant's visible appearance, and all-too-seldom is it followed by a truly rigorous chemical examination. Even when the chemical examination has been detailed, as in some more recent studies, the genetic analysis has of itself contributed little more than circumstantial evidence concerning secondary biosynthetic pathways, save in the very simplest cases.

The most complete studies have been concerned with the genetic regulation of flavonoid synthesis; for their biochemical interpretation they depend almost entirely on information based on other methods of study. For this reason, although some genetic evidence was used in presenting the description of flavonoid synthesis in Chapter Six (p. 88), no attempt is made to analyse such evidence here, though leading references are given on p. 92. In a way, it is perhaps unfortunate that so much genetic analysis has been concerned with flower pigmentation, since biochemically the flavonoids have been found to present a particularly complex example of the "grid problem". The different basic structures of flavonoids arise from a multiple-branched pathway, but can be varied independently in their oxygenation pattern, in methylation, in glycosylation, etc., while their manifestation in terms of flower colour is also profoundly influenced by cellular differentiation and by physiological controls (such as pH). Ironically, a considerable body of genetic analysis has also been concerned with the carotenoid pigmentation of plants, again with little effect on our knowledge of biosynthesis and, largely, for similar reasons. Perhaps some biosynthetic systems of less obvious nature, such as are now equally susceptible to detailed chemical analysis, would provide more suitable material with which this type of approach to biosynthetic information could be developed for higher plants.

FURTHER READING

General

R. P. Wagner and H. K. Mitchell, *Genetics and Metabolism*. (2nd ed.) Wiley, New York, 1964.

The Shikimic pathway

B. D. Davis, *Advances in Enzymology*, **16**, 247–312 (1955).
D. B. Sprinson, *Advances in Carbohydrate Chemistry*, **15**, 235–270 (1960).

Microbial metabolites

J. R. D. McCormick in Z. Vaněk and Z. Hošťálek (ed.) *Biogenesis of Antibiotic Substances*. Czechoslovak Academy of Sciences, Prague 1965.
M. Kikuchi and M. Nakahara, *Botanical Magazine* (*Tokyo*), **74**, 463–471 (1961).

Plant metabolites

R. E. Alston, in J. B. Harborne (ed.) *Biochemistry of Phenolic Compounds*. Academic, London, 1964, pp. 171–204 (phenolics generally).
J. B. Harborne in T. A. Geissman (ed.) *The Chemistry of Flavonoid Compounds*. Pergamon, Oxford, 1962, pp. 593–615 (flavonoids).

CHAPTER EIGHT

Alkaloids and other Amino-Acid Derivatives

The direct experimental study of alkaloid biogenesis, with which we are primarily concerned in this chapter, is a relatively recent aspect of alkaloid chemistry. Obvious requirements for its development were the availability of tracer substrates and of techniques for the separation and chemical degradation of complex alkaloids on a semi-micro scale; another essential prerequisite, however, was for the accumulation of a large body of purely speculative "biogenetic" hypotheses. Throughout this book the aim has been to emphasize those aspects of the subject which have substantial experimental basis, but particularly in a discussion of the alkaloids it would be misleading to omit notice of the role of hypotheses which, at the very least, have indicated the directions which experimental studies should follow when these became practicable. It has been the brilliant *a priori* reasoning of such pioneers as Trier and Robinson, and more recently of Barton, Woodward, Wenkert and others, which established the main outlines of our present picture of alkaloid biosynthesis; this inductive approach was based, first, on a very wide comparative study of alkaloid structures and, second, on chemical rationalizations in terms of the precursors thought likely to be found in plants and the reactions these might undergo *in vivo*.

In reasoning of this kind, every organic structure is seen as a coded summary of the processes by which it has been formed, and the first step in decoding is to identify common phrases in these messages, i.e. common features in a variety of structures which can be related to hypothetical precursors. In fact, the simplest kind of tracer incorporation experiment can be regarded simply as an aid to identifications of this kind. For example, the 3,4-dioxyphenylethylamine unit, shown in heavy type in the structure of thebaine (1), was first recognized inductively as a structural unit common to a very wide range of alkaloids, which moreover could be related to the known amino-acid 3,4-dihydroxyphenylalanine (2). The isolation of specifically-labelled thebaine from opium poppies after administering ^{14}C-labelled (2) merely made this identification more absolute. Only in more refined biogenetic studies has anything more than this confirmatory evidence been obtainable.

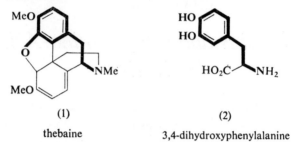

(1)   (2)

thebaine   3,4-dihydroxyphenylalanine

It was argued, as long ago as 1910, by Winterstein and Trier, that the alkaloids were derived principally from the amino-acids ornithine, lysine, phenylalanine, and tryptophane. Today we might add one or two other precursors to this list, point out many unsolved problems (some of the first importance), and add a motley collection of anomalous alkaloids of uncertain origin, but the original generalization is still sufficiently near the truth to provide, for example, the principal subheadings for this chapter. Despite the experimental work of the past ten years, our picture of the actual mechanisms of alkaloid synthesis often shows little more than a series of mechanistically plausible steps, which will explain the experimental data and will suggest further elaborations of hypothesis. The exact nature of the reacting species, the order of successive reactions, and the nature of the plant enzymes which confer structural and steric specificity throughout, remain for the most part quite unknown, and constitute one of the main objectives for future research. Against this, however, must be set the spectacular success of the inductive approach of "biogenetic thinking". Several thousand alkaloids of the most diverse structures have been grouped into biogenetically-defined classes, which enormously facilitate structural assignments in new and complex alkaloids, which have some taxonomic validity, and which have guided both the design and the interpretation of experimental studies of biogenesis.

Alkaloids based on Aliphatic Amino-acids

Pyrrolidines and related alkaloids contain C_4N units derived from the dibasic amino-acid ornithine; similarly, piperidine-type alkaloids contain C_5N units derived from lysine. The two groups show sufficiently close resemblances to be considered together, at least in outline, and some of the main experimental differences between them arise simply from the fact that, whereas ornithine is formed fairly directly

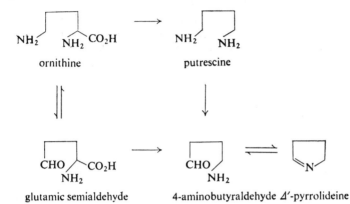

ornithine   putrescine

glutamic semialdehyde   4-aminobutyraldehyde Δ'-pyrrolideine

Figure 8.1. *Some pathways linking ornithine to 4-aminobutyraldehyde; similarly, lysine is converted into 5-aminopentanal/Δ^1-piperidine.*

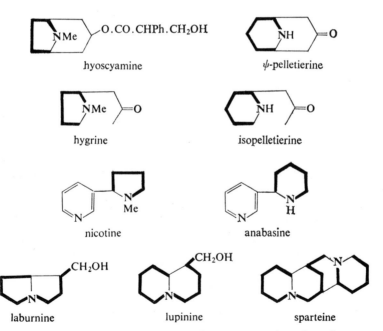

hyoscyamine ψ-pelletierine

hygrine   isopelletierine

nicotine   anabasine

laburnine   lupinine   sparteine

Figure 8.2. *Alkaloids known to contain lysine- or ornithine-derived units, arranged to show correspondences in the two series.*

from tricarboxylic acid cycle intermediates (via glutamic acid, by reduction) lysine biogenesis is more complex (and largely unknown). Both amino-acids are subject to decarboxylation and deamination processes, and the corresponding diamines putrescine and cadaverine are similarly effective in tracer experiments. Probably the actual alkaloid precursors are the γ- and δ-aminoaldehydes respectively, which are produced from the diamines by enzymic oxidation and are

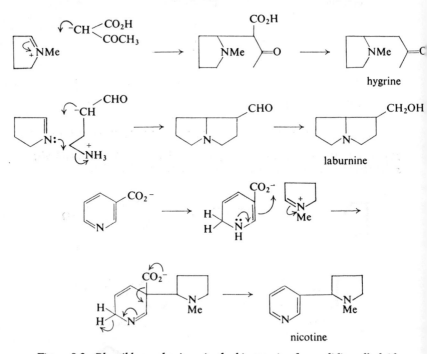

Figure 8.3. *Plausible mechanisms in the biogenesis of pyrrolidine alkaloids.*

normally in equilibrium with the cyclic imines (Figure 8.1); mechanistically most known assemblies could result from addition reactions of these compounds.

Figure 8.2 shows some corresponding alkaloids of the pyrrolidine and piperidine series, with the known C_4N or C_5N units in heavy type. In the tropine (hygrine etc.) and pelletierine series the remaining carbon atoms derive from acetoacetate, and in the nicotine alkaloids the pyridine ring derives from nicotinic acid (*see* below). The three alkaloid types illustrated can be derived by satisfactory mechanisms involving nucleophilic addition to the cyclic imines, as outlined in

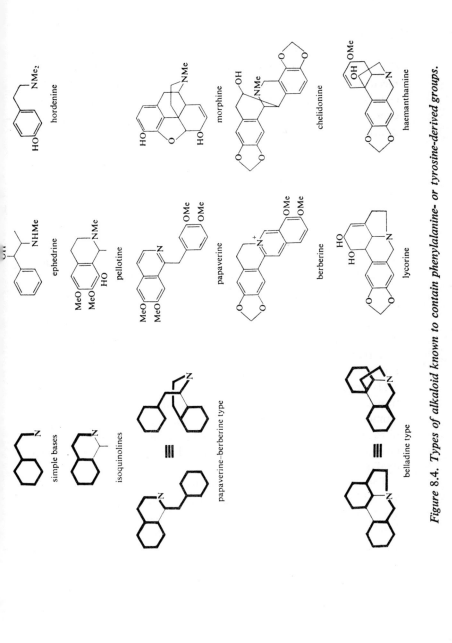

Figure 8.4. Types of alkaloid known to contain phenylalanine- or tyrosine-derived groups.

Figure 8.3 for those in the pyrrolidine series (corresponding mechanisms in the piperidine series appear equally feasible). Of these examples, only the cases of nicotine and anabasine require special comment; the similarity of the two rings in anabasine is entirely deceptive since they have entirely different origins. As shown in Figure 8.3, the pyridine ring of these alkaloids derives from nicotinic acid, and the suggested mechanism (which has some analogies with the action of nicotinamide coenzymes as hydride ion acceptors) is required to accommodate the experimental observations that in nicotine biosynthesis nicotinic acid undergoes decarboxylation and also hydrogen exchange at $C_{(6)}$.

The biogenesis of nicotinic acid in plants is known not to follow the pathway from tryptophane via kynurenine, which occurs in animals; rather, it arises from aspartic acid and glyceraldehyde, or from some closely-related compounds, but no details of the process are available.

Alkaloids based on Aromatic Amino-acids

The aromatic amino-acids phenylalanine and tyrosine, or their immediate precursors, are the parent compounds of an important range of alkaloids, in which they appear as variously-modified C_6C_2N (phenylethylamine) units; less directly these acids or their precursors afford other aromatic precursor units, notably of phenylacetaldehyde or benzaldehyde types. Both acids are formed from sugars, arising independently from the shikimic acid pathway, like anthranilic acid and tryptophane, which are also important alkaloid precursors. Phenylalanine can sometimes be converted into tyrosine, and both acids are subject to typical enzymic reactions of decarboxylation, transamination, imine formation etc., and to the direct elimination of ammonia to give the cinnamic acids on which a large number of non-nitrogenous metabolites are also based (Chapter Six). Moreover, the aromatic ring can be hydroxylated and the phenols can undergo oxidative coupling (cf. p. 36).

The interplay of such reactions gives rise to a great variety of alkaloids; the main types that have been investigated experimentally are shown in Figure 8.4, but to these we should add the far wider variety in which similar biogenetic origins are apparent on structural grounds alone. The five known types can be considered *seriatim* since they show increasing complexity.

Simple bases

Several simple phenylethylamine bases derive from phenylalanine or tyrosine (Figure 8.5). The sequence of reactions in hordenine bio-

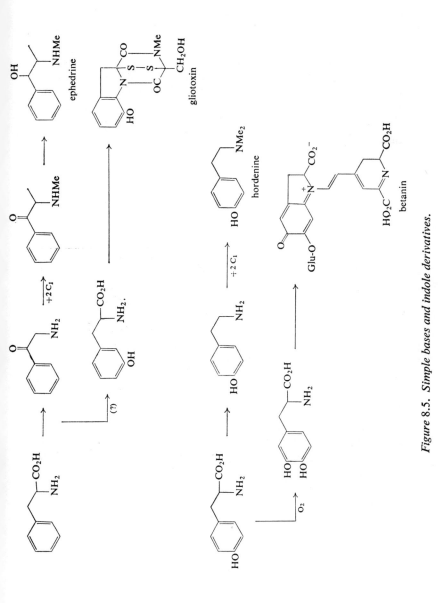

Figure 8.5. Simple bases and indole derivatives.

synthesis is fully established and has been correlated with the botanical development of the barley seedlings in which it occurs; ephedrine shows the additional complexity of C-alkylation by a methyl donor, and the sequence shown is partly conjectural. Betanin and gliotoxin exemplify more complex structures in which the C_6C_2N chain has been oxidatively cyclized to an indole derivative; the former compound is a plant pigment, almost certainly formed from tyrosine via 3,4-di-hydroxyphenylalanine, whereas the mould metabolite gliotoxin is formed from phenylalanine by way of *m*-tyrosine or, possibly, 2,3-dihydroxyphenylalanine.

Simple isoquinolines

The well-known *in vitro* reaction of suitably-oxygenated phenyl-ethylamines with aldehydes to give tetrahydroisoquinolines, e.g.

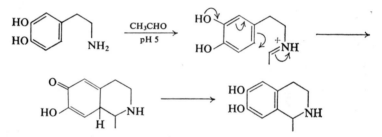

has for many years provided a plausible model for the origin of iso-quinoline alkaloids. Sometimes, as in pellotine (Figure 8.4), these are relatively simple (pellotine is formed from ^{14}C-tyrosine as expected), but in other cases the ensuing reactions complicate the picture (*see* below). Possibly *in vivo* the reacting entity is the pyridoxal derivative of the amino-acid, which is a normal intermediate in transamination, but which by a variant reaction with the aldehyde might afford the appropriate secondary imine.

Papaverine series

If an arylacetaldehyde is involved in isoquinoline formation, the product is a benzylisoquinoline such as papaverine; notable experimental work has been carried out in this series. Figure 8.6 shows some of the results in the series, including papaverine and the opium alkaloids. The parent base is norlaudanosoline, which is formed stereospecifically from two molecules of tyrosine via 3,4-dopa. One molecule affords 3,4-dihydroxyphenylethylamine, the other 3,4-dihydroxyphenylacetaldehyde or the equivalent pyruvic acid. From

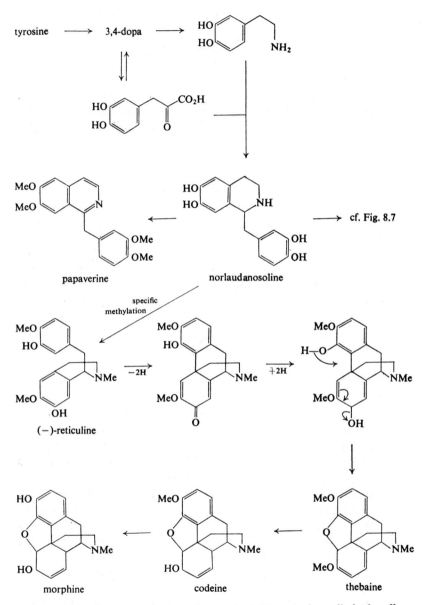

Figure 8.6. The papaverine/morphine series of isoquinoline alkaloids, all nor-laudanosoline derivatives.

norlaudanosoline, simple aromatization and O-alkylation suffice to form papaverine, while the thebaine-morphine alkaloids arise by the oxidative coupling process discussed more generally in Chapter Two (p. 36). Partial methylation of norlaudanosoline occurs in a specific manner, giving (−)-reticuline, and this limits the possibilities of the ensuing oxidation to the observed intramolecular *ortho-para* coupling. The ensuing sequence is based on an elegant combination of tracer studies and *in vitro* analogies and leads ultimately to morphine, as shown in Figure 8.6.

Berberine series

A further series of reticuline derivatives are the berberine-type alkaloids shown in Figure 8.7, distinguished for many years on *a priori* grounds because of the extra carbon atom now known to derive from methionine. Figure 8.7 shows the currently-favoured view that this "berberine bridge" is originally an *N*-methyl group, which alkylates the adjacent ring after an oxidation step; methylenedioxy groups similarly arise from *o*-methoxyphenols in the same system. In addition to berberine itself, Figure 8.7 also shows some alkaloids with modified ring-systems, whose biogenetic relationship was suspected on structural grounds and has now been confirmed, though without sequential details.

Belladine series

An interesting range of alkaloids from *Amaryllidaceae* (narcissus, etc.) shows several points of resemblance to the norlaudanosoline derivatives and has similarly been the object of very elegant experimental study. The hypothesis that they are formed by analogous types of oxidative coupling greatly facilitated structural elucidation in this series. Here the parent base (*see* Figure 8.8) is norbelladine, which contains a tyramine unit and a 3,4-dihydroxybenzaldehyde unit, joined by nitrogen as in norlaudanosoline. The tyramine is formed from tyrosine, and the 3,4-dihydroxybenzaldehyde unit arises from phenylalanine by way of cinnamic and caffeic acids (cf. Chapter Six). Oxidative coupling of the phenolic nuclei in different orientation provides a basic mechanism by which very diverse polycyclic systems are built up.

Some details of sequence shown in Figure 8.8 are based on direct experiment (e.g. that to tazettine); note how analogous reactions occur in each series, e.g. haemanthidine→tazettine and lycorine→hippeastrine. Some of the enzymes involved in the earlier stages have been

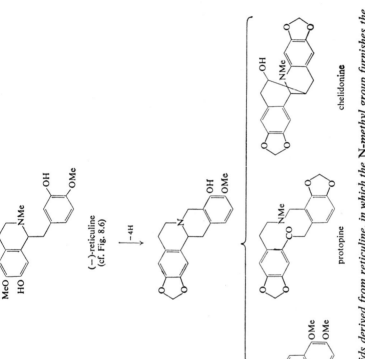

Figure 8.7. *Alkaloids derived from reticuline, in which the N-methyl group furnishes the extra carbon atom of the "berberine bridge" and O-methyl groups similarly afford methylenedioxy groups.*

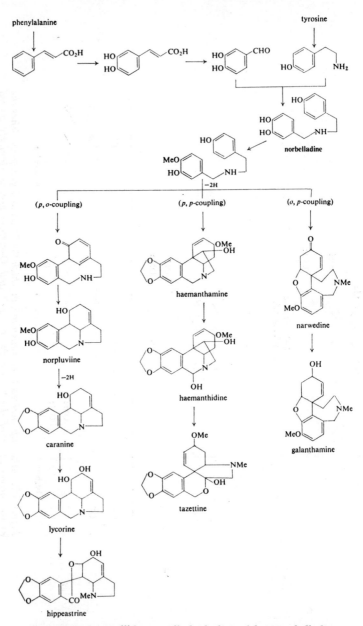

Figure 8.8. Amaryllidaceae *alkaloids derived from norbelladine.*

demonstrated to occur in appropriate tissue extracts, e.g. those effecting the deamination of phenylalanine and the methylation of norbelladine. In this series, unlike the norlaudanosoline series, the methylation step is clearly not sufficient to restrict subsequent oxidative coupling to a single course. Note also the oxidation step by which the methylenedioxy group of caranine is generated; this is believed to exemplify a general mechanism.

Alkaloids Derived from Tryptophane

In the "indole alkaloids", which are of considerable chemical and pharmacological interest, a tryptamine residue plays a similar role to

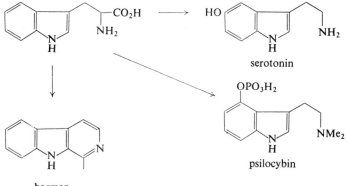

Figure 8.9. Simple tryptophane derivatives.

the phenylethylamine units already noted. Structural comparisons have been very successful in reducing this very large and complex series into some sort of order, which has been interpreted in considerable detail in terms of biogenetic hypothesis. The amount of successful experimental work in this field is, however, rather less.

Relatively simple indole bases are shown in Figure 8.9. Here serotonin—an animal hormone also found in some plants—and psilocybin, one of the hallucinogenic mushroom alkaloids, show the expected derivation from tryptophane, as do harman and related bases which are fully analogous to simpler isoquinolines. Several other indole alkaloid types show equally clear relationships to tryptamine but have not been studied experimentally. Tryptophane is also a precursor of the ergot alkaloids of *Claviceps* spp., produced either in infected cereals or in cultures. The parent skeleton is built up as shown in Figure 8.10, from tryptamine and mevalonate. The latter presumably

9

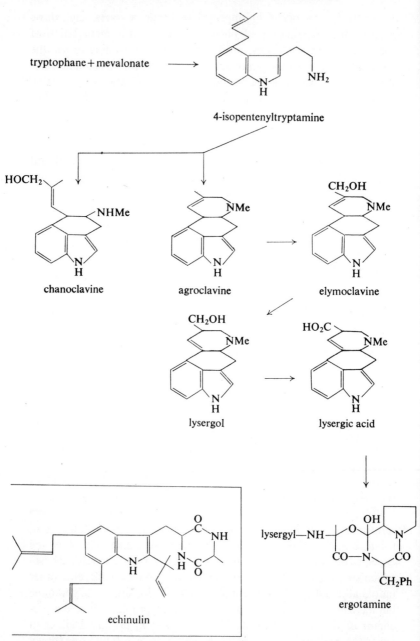

Figure 8.10. *Isopentenyl derivatives of tryptophane—the ergot alkaloids and echinulin.*

affords dimethylallyl pyrophosphate, which by alkylation probably generates 4-isopentenyltryptamine, though the identification of this as an intermediate is somewhat uncertain.

The alkaloids form a complex group (over 30 are known) and their interrelations are rather obscure, but tracer experiments suggest that agroclavine is the parent compound of the more important alkaloids,

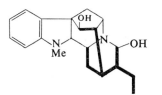

ajmaline

yohimbine

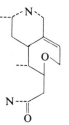

strychnine

cinchonamine

alstonine

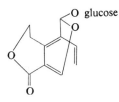

gentiopicrin

Figure 8.11. Indole alkaloids. The partial structures show typical forms taken by the non-indole moiety for comparison with the non-alkaloidal product gentiopicrin.

including lysergol and probably lysergic acid, while the tricyclic chanoclavine seems to be an alternative product from the parent isopentenyltryptophane. Lysergic acid itself is the parent compound of a series of amides, reaching the complexity of bases such as ergot-amine, which contains a cyclol structure derived from the tetrapeptide, lysergyl-alanyl-phenylalanyl-proline.

The course of isopentenylation in *Claviceps* spp. forms an interesting comparison with that seen in echinulin, another fungal metabolite also shown in Figure 8.10, in which mevalonate-derived groups have been attached to the indole nucleus at $C_{(5)}$, $C_{(7)}$, and $C_{(3)}$ or indole-N, the last-mentioned having then undergone rearrangement to give the unusual 1,1-dimethylallyl group at $C_{(2)}$.

In the largest, and at present most perplexing group of indole alkaloids, the tryptamine unit is combined in various ways with a second skeletal fragment of unknown origin. Figure 8.11 shows one alkaloid of this type, ajmaline, together with partial formulae showing the same fragment as found in several other alkaloids of the series; also shown is one example of the occurrence of this unit in a non-alkaloidal plant product. The tryptamine unit has been identified experimentally (e.g. in ajmaline), but for the other unit there exists only some contradictory and inconclusive data. In hypothetical schemes this unit has been derived by rearrangements of a terpenoid skeleton, of phenylalanine, or of a prephenic acid derivative, or from a non-linear assembly of "acetate", "malonate", and "formate" units. Recent work shows conclusively that the C_{10} units arise from terpenoids of the iridodial type (cf. p. 63).

Among these complex indole alkaloids are many apparent examples of further transformations of the initial biogenetic product, as in the morphine series etc., but few have been studied experimentally. An interesting exception is provided by the quinine alkaloids shown in Figure 8.12. On inductive grounds, cinchonamine was plausibly derived from a precursor of the type shown (cf. also, Figure 8.11), and cinchonine, from the same plant source, was then hypothetically derived by opening the indole ring and recyclization as indicated. Experimentally, the location of labelling in quinine (methoxy-cinchonine) derived from α-^{14}C-tryptophane, which as shown in Figure 8.12 is somewhat remarkable, provided welcome confirmation of a far-sighted hypothesis.

Other Alkaloids

Because of recent experimental work it has been possible in this chapter at least to mention the main alkaloid groups, though not always to an extent commensurate with their importance. Several minor groups of alkaloids have escaped mention, e.g. derivatives of steroids and of lower terpenoids, alkaloids derived from anthranilic acid, colchicine, etc. Many others can be classified biogenetically by hypothesis but still await experimental study. As a class, the alkaloids raise interesting problems concerning the interplay of specific and non-specific reactions in secondary biosynthesis. Thus, our Figures 8.6 to 8.8 show in a very simplified form how a few specific processes determine the general course of biosynthesis and are then diversified almost indefinitely by further transformations of a less specific nature. The situation is not confined to alkaloid biosynthesis.

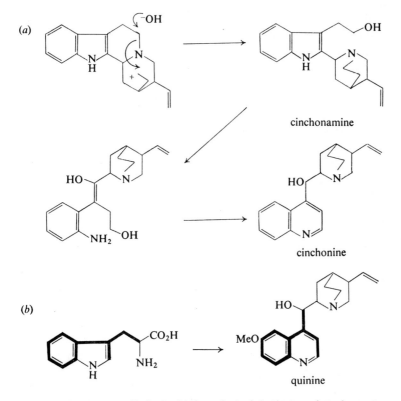

Figure 8.12. Quinine alkaloids: (a) *hypothetical derivation of cinchonamine and cinchonine,* (b) *tryptamine skeleton as found experimentally in quinine.*

Other Amino-acid Derivatives

In interest and importance, and also by sheer number and variety, the plant alkaloids tend to dominate our ideas concerning secondary metabolites of amino-acids. Nevertheless, there are other important categories derived from the amino-acids, especially in fungi and bacteria that rarely produce alkaloids. These further categories show considerable variety, and their secondary status is not always clear our knowledge of their biosynthesis is very incomplete. It is convenient to consider peptide derivatives separately.

Modified amino-acids

Non-peptide metabolites derived from amino-acids include the plant alkaloids already discussed, and the nitrogen-free phenylpropane derivatives of Chapter Six. There is also a series of uncommon amino-acids not involved in protein structure and with a restricted occurrence, mainly in higher plants; unfortunately, we know rather little of their biochemistry. Unusual modifications of common amino-acids are seen in azaserine, cycloserine, and β-nitropropionic acid (from β-alanine). These are shown in Figure 8.13 together with the antibiotic chloramphenicol, which presumably derives from an aromatic amino-acid, though its structure has so far resisted biogenetic analysis. More complex heterocycles include the pigment prodigiosin (Figure 8.13), in which the two fragments which combine in the last step of biosynthesis are themselves derived from glycine, proline, and acetate, in an unknown manner.

Polymeric quinoid pigments (melanins) are widely-distributed in plants and animals, and are formed *in situ* by oxidative polymerizations within a cellular matrix. Best-known are those formed from tyrosine by way of indole-5,6-quinone (Figure 8.14); this quinone, and polymers derived from it, readily combine with amino- and sulphydryl-groups of proteins, so that the polymeric pigment can also have a structural role. Similar uses are made of the oxidation of other phenols, especially in insects and other invertebrate animals, and sometimes the related monomeric quinones may accumulate. Often these compounds are derived from tyrosine; homogentisic acid is one example, and another is N-acetyl-dihydroxyphenylethylamine (N-acetyldopamine). Thus, in blowfly larvae, tyrosine is largely metabolized via p-hydroxyphenylpyruvic acid, but at pupation, under hormonal influence, metabolism is switched to N-acetyldopamine production, oxidation of this phenol then providing a cross-linking and pigmenting agent for the pupal case. In other insect tissues proteins are cross-linked by direct *ortho*-coupling of tyrosine residues. Yet another type of insect pigment is the ommochromes, which are monomeric and polymeric phenoxazines derived from 3-hydroxykynurenine, itself a breakdown product of tryptophane.

An alternative type of reaction involving tyrosine leads to a 3-amino-coumarin, as in the antibiotic novobiocin (Figure 8.15). This is an excellent example of mixed biogenesis with units deriving from glucose

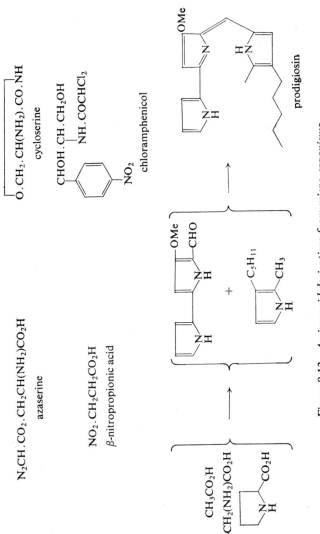

Figure 8.13. Amino-acid derivatives from micro-organisms.

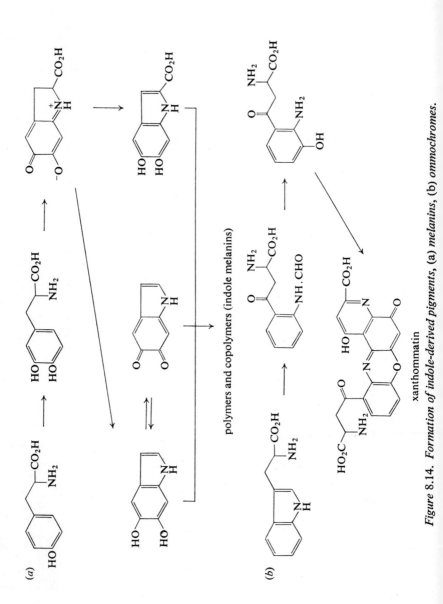

Figure 8.14. Formation of indole-derived pigments, (a) melanins, (b) ommochromes.

(noviose), tyrosine (coumarin and *p*-hydroxybenzoate), methionine (O- and C-methyl groups), and mevalonate (isopentenyl group).

The formation of ommochromes from hydroxykynurenine is paralleled by the formation of other phenazines and phenoxazines from anthranilic acids (Figure 8.16). The phenazine pigment chlororaphin, from *Pseudomonas* sp., is at least partly derived from anthranilic acid, while the fungal pigment cinnabarinic acid and the phenoxazine nucleus of actinomycin clearly derive from 3-hydroxy-anthranilate; in actinomycin the C-methyl groups are introduced from methionine, and the oxidative condensation probably involves the appropriate anthranilyl-peptide derivatives. A somewhat different structural type is viridicatin, a fungal metabolite formed from anthranilic acid and the C_6C_3 unit of phenylalanine (Figure 8.16).

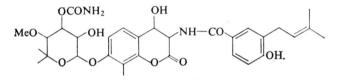

Figure 8.15. Novobiocin, a streptomycete antibiotic of "mixed" biogenesis.

Peptide Derivatives

Oligopeptide derivatives of considerable variety occur as bacterial and fungal metabolites, and a few are shown in Figure 8.17. Thus, from fungi come the penicillins, which are modified tripeptides, and fungisporin, a spore component, as well as phytotoxic peptides such as lycomarasmin (cf. also the peptide moiety of ergot alkaloids, Figure 8.10). From streptomycetes come such antibiotics as the actinomycins (Figure 8.16) or valinomycin, a "peptolide", while bacteria produce a range of peptide antibiotics exemplified by bacitracin-A. Structurally, such peptides differ from proteins by several orders of magnitude and are generally smaller than the animal hormones. Nearly all contain features absent in proteins—amino-acids of novel structure or configuration, or special structural modifications. Identification of the component amino-acids seldom presents difficulties, but beyond this our knowledge of the biosynthesis of these compounds is rather scanty, and on the important question of its relationship to protein biosynthesis the evidence is somewhat conflicting.

It should be noted that the distinction between "primary" and

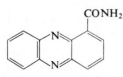

chororaphin

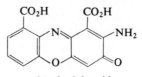

cinnabarinic acid

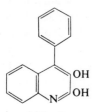

viridicatin

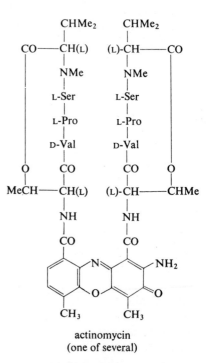

actinomycin
(one of several)

Figure 8.16. Derivatives of anthranilic acids.

"secondary" metabolites is not always easily made in this group. Such a typical extracellular antibiotic as bacitracin is also a functional component of the spore-walls, and we may suspect a similar role for fungisporin. Species-differences between bacteria are also associated with some cell-wall substances of this type, containing D-amino-acid residues. Thus, teichoic acids contain D-alanine, while in *Staphylococ-*

cus aureus the muramic acid is linked to a pentapeptide with D-alanyl and D-glutamyl units (Figure 8.18).

The biosynthesis of actinomycin is stated to be a separate process from protein synthesis, and the two compete for common amino-acids. The nature of any differences from protein synthesis is, however,

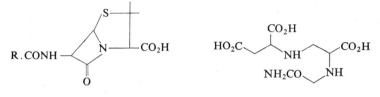

penicillins   *lycomarasmin*

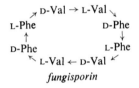

fungisporin

D-Val → L-Lac → L-Val → D-αHOisovaleryl → D-Val → L-Lac
　↑　　　　　　　　　　　　　　　　　　　　　　　　↓
D-αHOisovaleryl ← L-Val ← L-Lac ← D-Val ← D-αHOisovaleryl ← L-Val

valinomycin

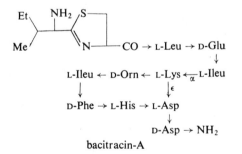

bacitracin-A

Figure 8.17. *Some oligopeptide antibiotics.*

uncertain. One key step in protein synthesis is the formation of amino-acyl adenylates from ATP with pyrophosphate elimination. The analogous step in oligopeptide synthesis sometimes involves phosphate elimination (e.g. the activation of γ-glutamylcysteine for glutathione synthesis or of L-lysine for incorporation into muramic acids), while in other cases no comparable reaction could be demonstrated. The characteristic D-amino-acid residues are sometimes stated to arise only from incorporation of the normal L-isomers. For example, L-valine labels the D- and L-valyl and the D-α-hydroxy-isovaleryl units of valinomycin and the D-valyl units of actinomycin, and only L-ornithine is incorporated into bacitracin. However, in a *cell-free* preparation from *B. subtilis*, D- and L-valine were said to be separately and specifically incorporated into the corresponding units of oligopeptide antibiotics (gramicidin and tyrothricin) and of protein.

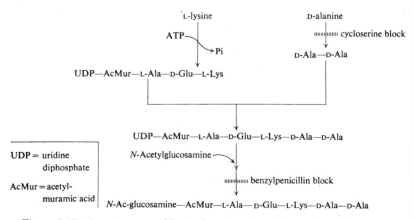

Figure 8.18. *Stepwise assembly of the muramic acid peptide in* S. aureus.

Comparison with later stages of protein synthesis also raises contradictions. Thus, in *B. licheniformis*, chloramphenicol has no effect on bacitracin synthesis though it interferes with protein synthesis at the transfer-RNA stage. On the other hand, each antibiotic synthesis in the *B. subtilis* cell-extract was said to require the full complement of appropriate amino-acids for each antibiotic and to be blocked by the absence of any one of them, while the synthesis required ATP and was carried out by a combination of ribosome and "soluble" fractions; such a picture would seem closely parallel to the requirements for protein synthesis. One important difference between the biosynthesis of peptide antibiotics and that of proteins is typical of secondary biosynthesis in general, namely, the lower specificity of the secondary processes. In many cases, individual amino-acids of the peptide may be replaced by one of several others, simply according to their immediate availability; mixtures of related peptides are thus produced and their precise composition can be influenced by external factors. By contrast, the "recognition" of amino-acids in protein synthesis is exceedingly precise.

As shown in Figure 8.18, the muramic acid derivative from *S. aureus* is assembled stepwise, from UDP-acetylmuramic acid, L-lysine, and D-alanyl-D-alanine; note the different points at which this synthesis is blocked by cycloserine and benzylpenicillin, both antibiotics which are active against *S. aureus*.

Some details of the biosynthetic sequence are also known for the penicillins (Figure 8.19). Here the precursor is a tripeptide formed

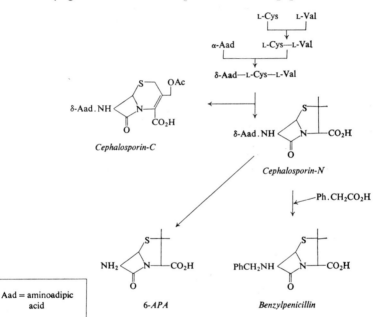

Figure 8.19. *Assembly sequence in biosynthesis of penicillins.*

from α-aminoadipate and L-cysteinyl-L-valine. D-Valine inhibits the synthesis (though in the penicillins the valyl residue has this configuration) and $^{14}C, ^{15}N$-L-valine is incorporated intact in short-term experiments. The α-aminoadipate is also a lysine precursor, and lysine inhibits penicillin synthesis by a "feedback" effect. The tripeptide may then undergo oxidative cyclization; the mechanism of this step has been repeatedly discussed and it is known to involve inversion of configuration of the valine unit and retention of the α-hydrogen and one β-hydrogen of the cysteine. Two alternative cyclization products are produced in *Cephalosporium* spp., namely, cephalosporin-C and -N; in *Penicillium* spp. the latter undergoes either hydrolysis tc 6-aminopenicillanic acid, or ester exchange with a variety of acids supplied to the cultures, e.g. with phenylacetic acid to give benzyl-penicillin.

FURTHER READING

Alkaloids

R. Robinson, *The Structural Relations of Natural Products*. Clarendon, Oxford, 1955.

A. Battersby, *Proc. chem. Soc.*, **1963**, 189–200.

K. Mothes and H. R. Schutte, *Angewandte Chemie* (*International Edition*), **2**, 341–357; 441–458 (1963).

D. H. R. Barton, *Proc. chem. Soc.*, 1963, 293–198.

E. Leete, in P. Bernfeld (ed.) *The Biogenesis of Natural Compounds*. Pergamon, Oxford, 1963, pp. 739–798.

Other products

J. H. Birkinshaw and C. E. Stickings, *Fortschritte der Chemie organischer Naturstoffe*, **20**, 1–40 (1962) (nitrogenous compounds from fungi).

M. Bodanszky and D. Perlman, *Nature*, **204**, 840–844 (1964) (peptide antibiotics).

Articles by E. P. Abraham (penicillins) and E. Katz (actinomycins) in Z. Vaněk and Z. Hošťálek (ed.) *Biogenesis of Antibiotic Substances*. Czechoslovak Academy of Sciences, Prague 1965.

CHAPTER NINE

Precursor Experiments in Higher Plants

The range of natural products from higher plants is considerably greater than that of fungal products, and their structures are equally amenable to biogenetic hypothesis, yet our *experimental* knowledge of secondary metabolism in higher plants is comparatively meagre. The situation is well displayed with terpenoid compounds; far more is known about the biogenesis of a few, rather atypical, terpenoids from fungi than about the enormous and important series of plant isoprenoids. Reasons for this disparity lie in the special circumstances which hinder simple precursor-incorporation experiments in higher plants.

Obviously, the higher plants are far more complex systems than any micro-organism. Consequences of their polyploid constitution and autotrophic nutrition were considered in Chapter Seven; here we are concerned with their structural and dynamic complexity, at all levels up to the macroscopic. These multicellular organisms have differently-constituted organic parts, all held in complex interdependence. During their whole lifetime they undergo continuous growth, development, and differentiation. In relation to secondary metabolism, this means that a particular substance may be synthesized only in a particular part of the plant, at a particular stage of its development and at a particular time in the life-history and seasonal progression of the plant. Clearly, the study of such a synthesis requires the right material at the right time. However, for the whole of a synthetic process these desiderata may be impossible; a synthesis may be initiated in one part of the plant at one time and continued elsewhere at a later date.

Some of these circumstances have been strikingly displayed by Wilson and co-workers (*see* p. 141), who have exploited the changes in atmospheric ^{14}C content in recent years due to bomb testing. The ^{14}C content of a plant constituent gives an indication of the date at which the carbon in that constituent was removed from the pool of intermediates which are in radiochemical equilibrium with photosynthesis products. In the *Pinus* spp. studied, in which sapwood cells develop into heartwood some 10–12 years after they are first formed, the cellulose in an annual growth ring retains the ^{14}C content of the year in which the ring was first formed. So also do the heartwood extractives (mainly phenylpropanoid phenolics), despite the fact that these do not occur as such in the sapwood zones, i.e. these characteristic heartwood components arise from sapwood constituents which have been "out of circulation" since the growth zone was first formed. On the other hand, the resin constituents (mainly isoprenoids) of the same growth rings show signs of more prolonged equilibration with the photosynthetic pool. In tea plants, the carbon of caffeine (a purine) is removed from the equilibrium pool some six months before the development of the leaf-bud in which the caffeine itself is formed. It must be remembered that the photosynthetic process occurs in the green parts of the plant, and feeds into a complex transport system. Circulating materials pass from photosynthesis sites to growing-points (meristem tissue) and to storage organs (e.g. root depots), and also, independently, from storage sites to growing-points. Such transport is partly a passive circulation and partly an active process, mediated against osmotic gradients by special mechanisms which are ultimately enzymic and capable of chemical specificity.

The difficulty of selecting the correct plant part is of major importance in examining a biosynthetic pathway. It can, of course, be avoided—or rather ignored—by using the whole plant, a technique which can give useful results but which some authors find unconvincing (*see* below). We have seen that the site at which a product is most obviously to be found is not necessarily that at which it is actually synthesized. As a generalization it may be taken that the most active centres of secondary biosynthesis in plants are very often the regions of growth; more precisely, the regions immediately behind the most active meristem cells. This has been demonstrated for a variety of alkaloids and plant phenolics; however, this is not necessarily the site at which the final products are formed since further transformations may occur selectively in other parts of the plant. For example, in some *Nicotiana* spp. nicotine is formed in the growing roots but is transported to the leaves, where it is demethylated to nornicotine. Morphine alkaloids are produced very rapidly by germinating poppy seeds but the mixture of products is not that found in the mature plant. In mint, terpenes are mainly synthesized in the early leaf bud, but the conversion of menthol into menthone seems to occur as the leaves mature. Betaine formation from tyramine in barley occurs only in the very young sprouting shoot, but the corresponding reaction of proline, in alfalfa, occurs only in older plants.

Germinating seeds have proved especially well suited for biosynthetic studies in a variety of cases. One reason is their obvious experimental convenience—acorns are easier to slice than oak-trees and come in standard sizes—and another is that many characteristic plant products are first formed in the germinating embryo. For example, the stepwise methylation of tyramine to hordenine is carried out by enzymes formed inductively in the first period after sprouting. The characteristic polyacetylenes of Compositae, or the alkaloids of poppies, are absent from the seeds but present in very small seedlings. Such material thus offers the desired synthetic system in a relatively "concentrated" form. Moreover, these early stages of plant development occur prior to the appearance of the photosynthetic apparatus (this can be delayed by keeping the seedlings in the dark). Photosynthesis inevitably leads to a considerable dilution of any administered ^{14}C compounds by carbon incorporated from CO_2, and also opens up pathways by which many specifically-labelled substances become rapidly randomized. Also, the specialized development of photosynthetic apparatus in the chloroplasts represents a major complication of the plant material—*see*, for example, the compartmentalization effects noted in Chapter Four (p. 67). Photosynthesis can also lead to the setting-up of diurnal rhythms in the carbon flow, or in reducing power, etc., which can have considerable effects in many biosynthetic sequences.

Interesting and informative work on triterpenoid synthesis (*see* Chapter Four) in germinating peas has been described by Nes and co-workers (*see* p. 141). If $2\text{-}^{14}C$-mevalonate is added to the water used to bring about germination, it is completely taken up by the peas in a few hours, which itself is an important matter. Twenty-four hours after germination, nearly 40 per cent of the ^{14}C supplied as D-mevalonate is present as squalene, while four days later the squalene is barely active, but over 45 per cent of the ^{14}C is present in the cyclization product, β-amyrin. These incorporation figures are, of course, extremely high and correspondingly convincing; the fact that on the fifth day only some 2 per cent of the ^{14}C is found in β-sitosterol (the major sterol of the seedlings) thus gives a direct demonstration that the pathway to such a sterol from squalene is far less direct than the one-step cyclization to β-amyrin. Another interesting observation made with this material is that if the mevalonate is supplied in large excess, instead of in tracer amounts, there is a gross accumulation of squalene, which

10

even on the fifth day still contains 40 per cent of the ^{14}C. This indicates that, while mevalonate synthesis is normally the slowest reaction in the system, when this limiting step is by-passed, the next slowest step is not in the synthesis of squalene but in its cyclization. Information of this kind is not normally so readily accessible in intact organisms.

For reactions which are peculiar to more mature plants, other techniques must be used. The complicating effect of photosynthesis has already been noted; a simple example is the considerable dilution of acetate, e.g. in the phloroglucinol ring of flavonoids, during photosynthesis. On the other hand, photosynthetic incorporation of $^{14}CO_2$ has its own uses; it is particularly valuable as an indication of "whole-plant" activity, though seldom affording much chemical detail. Short exposures to $^{14}CO_2$ of high activity can be used to pick out some sequential details by observing subsequent levels in particular constituents (e.g. in the thebaine–codeine–morphine series) and to reveal the relative pool sizes in different reaction series. Prolonged photosynthesis in $^{14}CO_2$ is mainly used to obtain uniformly labelled natural products for other experiments.

If we combine the considerations already outlined with those discussed for precursor-incorporation experiments in micro-organisms in Chapter Three, the general protocols for such experiments in plants follow. Precursors can be administered in a variety of ways, depending upon their nature and on the plant material selected. In some early work, plants were simply exposed to the vapour of certain non-natural materials such as ethylene chlorhydrin or hydroquinone, which were effectively converted into glycosides (thus demonstrating the presence of rather general glycosylation enzymes). Labelled precursors supposedly related to natural intermediates have been fed to whole plants by supplying them in aqueous solution (of suitable pH) to the roots, by painting them on the leaves, by direct injection into stems or other suitable parts, or via a "wick" threaded into the plant, *etc.* Besides the general limitations already discussed, such methods vary considerably in their efficiency. One complication of root feeding is that compounds may be rapidly absorbed from solution by root hairs without passing at any corresponding rate into the rest of the plant. When administered to plants thus generally, many compounds may have very undesirable effects. This is found not only with compounds which are not normal plant constituents, e.g. geranic acid, which is toxic down to 1 in 10^4 dilutions and could not be examined as a terpene precursor, but also with normal plant constituents, especially if these are usually present only in minute amounts. For example, it is difficult to test nicotinic acid as a nicotine precursor because of its hormone-like effects; equally it is difficult to investigate the metabolism of gibberellic acid in normal plants. Even simple compounds such as acetate or succinate can cause marked changes in the balance of synthetic and degradative processes in the tricarboxylic acid cycle. When the compound is normally present in limiting amounts there is the added danger that any increase in its concentration can lead to the induction of new enzymes effecting abnormal transformations.

A variety of larger plant parts has also been used in precursor-incorporation studies. Twigs or single leaves can be detached and the cut ends immersed in tracer solutions, tissue slices can be used, or discs can be cut from leaves and floated on the tracer solution. Such methods are experimentally convenient, since the plant material is so easily manipulated, and such plant material may often contain a somewhat higher proportion of relevant tissue than would the whole plant. However, the diluting effect of irrelevant processes is usually very great, and although these methods have been very usefully employed, for example in studies of alkaloid biosynthesis, better techniques are generally desirable. Increasing attention is being given to the use of plant tissue cultures in biosynthetic investigations for this reason. Provided the reaction in question is one carried out by the tissue culture the method has obvious advantages; on the other hand, the laboratory techniques for plant tissue culture are often somewhat more demanding than those which may suffice for micro-organisms. Principally this is because the plant tissue culture is deprived of the regulated environment offered by the whole plant.

A comparison of different techniques can be made using various published data for the incorporation of precursors into alkaloids of the morphine and Amaryllidaceae series. These results are not necessarily the best that could be obtained, but are typical of data regarded as significant or as a basis for further operations. By root-feeding of whole plants, incorporations of ^{14}C-tyrosine of the order of 0·01 to 0·1 per cent were obtained, while direct injection into seedpods at the time when alkaloids were forming there gave incorporations of 2–4 per cent. Compounds not regarded as precursors gave incorporations lower by factors of 10–100. Specialized intermediates in a biosynthetic pathway gave higher incorporations, e.g. norpluviine to lycorine, up to 10 per cent; thebaine to codeine and morphine, up to 12 per cent. However, these latter figures are scarcely so high as the reaction systems would seem to require (*see* Figures 8.6 and 8.8), and suggest that a large part of the administered intermediate alkaloid was being retained before reaching the site of transformation. For reasons of this kind, it may be thought preferable to record the extent to which the administered precursor undergoes dilution during its incorporation into the product being investigated. When this is done, dilutions of several thousandfold, or even greater, are commonly found in experiments with whole plants, whereas in parallel experiments using suitable tissue cultures dilutions of only a few hundred have been observed.

Clearly, the use of plant tissue cultures, wherever possible, offers considerable advantages. They can be obtained from a variety of plant, parts, provided these are characterized by rapid growth, e.g. root tips, seed endosperm, floral primordia, etc. Some disadvantages are that only a part of a biosynthetic sequence may be realizable in a particular tissue, and, conversely, that the activity of the tissue in culture may be somewhat modified from that in the intact plant. Because of the lack of regulation effects, the tissue culture may also be more easily "upset". In future work we may expect more general use of the tissue culture method, interpreting the results with due regard to these limitations, and perhaps leading to a direct study of the regulation effects themselves, as operative in the entire plant. Such work would add considerably to our understanding, not only of secondary biosynthesis, but also of the dynamic chemical organization of higher plants.

Interpretation — the Morphine Alkaloids

Because the subject has attracted attention from several groups of workers, with different conceptual approaches, some aspects of the biosynthesis of morphine alkaloids suitably illustrate points of interpretation in precursor-incorporation experiments. The biogenetic situation has already been outlined in Chapter Eight (Figure 8.6). In particular, it is seen there that

(1) the carbon skeleton is contributed by two dihydroxy-phenylethyl (C_6C_2) units, which are first seen combined with the nitrogen atom in norlaudanosoline;

(2) the principal alkaloids thebaine, codeine, and morphine are formed in that sequence.

Both these aspects have been studied, and interpreted in somewhat varying ways, which can profitably be examined (references to original papers, p. 141).

Most of the tracer studies have used ^{14}C-tyrosine as the test precursor. Free tyrosine is present in the plants, and normally the added

[14]C-tyrosine is incorporated with nearly equal efficiency into both of the C_6C_2 units. This is the principal item of direct evidence for the mode of formation of norlaudanosoline. Only in a naïve sense, however, does it imply that, e.g. "the morphine alkaloids are formed from

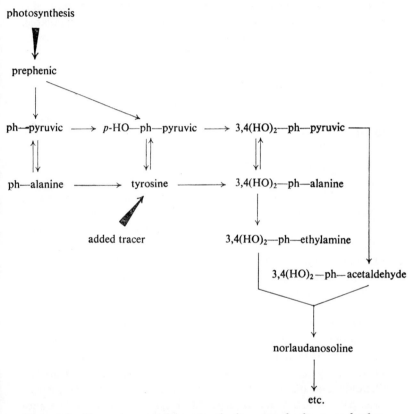

Figure 9.1. *Illustrating part of the network of reactions leading to norlaudanosoline, in which the paths of carbon from photosynthesis products and from tyrosine are only partly coincident.*

two molecules of tyrosine". Suppose that, for the sake of argument, we accept the simple hypothesis that the norlaudanosoline is actually formed from one molecule of 3,4-dihydroxyphenylethylamine and one of 3,4-dihydroxyphenylacetaldehyde, as in model reactions *in vitro*. Some of the relevant compounds and reactions are then as shown in Figure 9.1. All the compounds shown there also enter, to varying degrees, into other competing reactions which are not shown. Moreover, the reactions shown do not all proceed at comparable rates, the pools of intermediates are not all of equal sizes, and the compounds do not all diffuse within the plant at equal rates. We can then see from the figure that the main flow of carbon in the plant is normally from photosynthesis and enters via prephenic acid, but after that point it is not definable without quantitative data, which are not easily available. If, however, we compare the flow of carbon from added ^{14}C-tyrosine we can see immediately that the two will only partly coincide.

Experimentally it is found that in short-term experiments, photosynthetically incorporated $^{14}CO_2$ tends to enter one C_6C_2 unit of the morphine alkaloids more rapidly than the other, and this has been considered as an argument against the evidence from tyrosine incorporation. In fact, we must accept that the symmetrical incorporation observed with ^{14}C-tyrosine seems to arise from the redistribution between intermediates which can occur in longer-term experiments, and is partly coincidental, since in some related alkaloids, a less symmetrical incorporation of tyrosine itself has been observed. Nevertheless, it is the experiments with ^{14}C-tyrosine, and not those with $^{14}CO_2$, which yield the primary information as to the general pathway of the alkaloid synthesis. Conversely, the $^{14}CO_2$ experiments do nothing to invalidate this information, though they might lead to some improved knowledge of the details of Figure 9.1.

The conversion sequence thebaine–codeine–morphine, which seems at first sight to be in the opposite direction to that expected, since it involves the removal of O-methyl groups, was first proposed to explain precursor experiments in which administered tracer appeared most rapidly in thebaine, then in codeine, and most slowly in morphine. Subsequently the conversions were demonstrated directly with labelled alkaloids, and other experiments, which indicated that the methylation pattern first established in the biosynthesis from norlaudanosoline is that of thebaine, afforded confirmation of a different kind. In time-course experiments, the incorporation data for thebaine, codeine and morphine agreed qualitatively with the predicted behaviour for such a series (cf. Chapter Three), but in later quantitative studies several differences from the theoretical case were observed. Using ^{14}C-tyrosine as precursor, it was found, first, that substantial quantities of unlabelled carbon were simultaneously entering the alkaloids and diluting their activity, and second, that incorporation into morphine never rose to levels corresponding to the total turnover of ^{14}C in thebaine.

As already noted, the first of these observations is scarcely surprising, and indeed the observed dilutions of ^{14}C show effects which would be expected to result from the diurnal variations of photosynthetic activity. The second observation would present serious difficulties only if the sequence

$$precursor \rightarrow thebaine \rightarrow codeine \rightarrow morphine$$

were a closed one, and codeine and morphine were the only metabolites of thebaine. In fact, this is very unlikely; even if we disregard compartmentalization and diffusion effects, a number of closely-related alkaloids are also present and at least some of these must represent alternative metabolites of thebaine. Under such circumstances the theoretical analyses which deal with simple precursor-product relationships are quantitatively inadequate. Once again, a full account would require details of the relative rates of all the competing reactions, and such data are not available.

As a general principle, it may be argued that, given the real complexity of secondary biosynthetic systems, their analysis by the precursor-incorporation method is only possible because the method itself is not over-refined. Consequently the results obtained have a broad truth which is unaffected by the lack of resolution of finer details. As in optics, if we attempt too high a magnification, the image disappears.

FURTHER READING

General

A. T. Wilson *et al.*, *Nature*, **204**, 73 (1964); **198**, 500 (1963); **197**, 711 (1963).

R. J. Suhadolnik, A. G. Fischer and J. Zulalian, *Biochem. Biophys. Res. Comm.*, **11**, 208 (1963) (floral primordia, etc.)

D. R. Christman and R. F. Dawson, *Biochemistry*, **2**, 182 (1963) (exercised root cultures and steady-state conditions).

W. R. Nes *et al.*, *Biochemistry*, **1**, 537, 1178 (1962) (triterpenoids in germinating seeds).

Morphine alkaloids

A. Battersby, R. Binks and B. J. Harper, *J. Chem. Soc.*, **1962**, 3526, 3534.

F. R. Stermitz and H. Rapoport, *J. Amer. chem. Soc.*, **83**, 4298 (1961).

S. Gross and R. F. Dawson, *Biochemistry*, **2**, 185 (1963).

J. W. Fairbairn, A. Paterson and G. Wassel, *Phytochemistry*, **3**, 577, 583, (1964).

Subject Index

A

Acetoacetyl-CoA, formation of, 15, 46
  as precursor, 6, 26, 27, 47, 63, 100, 110, 112
Acetyl-CoA, formation of, 6, 14
  as precursor, 13–37
N-Acetyldopamine, 124
Acetylenes, 20–22
Actinomycins, 127–130
Adenosine triphosphate, importance of, 8
S-Adenosylmethionine—
  alkylation by, 7
    of alkaloids, 100–104
    of fatty acids, 18–21
    of polyketides, 29–31
    of terpenoids, 65–66
Aesculetin, 81–82
Agroclavine, 49, 120–121
Ajmaline, 121–122
Alanine, formation of, 6
  (*see also* peptides)
Alfalfa, betaines formed in, 135
Alkylation (*see* S-Adenosylmethionine, 3,3-Dimethylallyl pyrophosphate)
Allylbenzene derivatives, 83
Alstonine, 121
Alternariol, 28
Amaryllidaceae, alkaloids of, 116, 118–119, 137
Amino-acids, formation of, 6
  unusual, 124–125
  in peptides, 127–130
α-Aminoadipic acid, 131–132
P-Aminobenzoic acid, formation, 79
  requirement for, 95
6-Aminopenicillanic acid (6-APA), 132

β-Amyrin, 61–62
  in peas, 135
Anabasine, 112
Anhydrorhodovibrin, 67–68
Anthranilic acid, formation of, 79
  as precursor, 122, 127–128
  requirement for, 96
Anthraquinones, 26–27, 34–36, 101, 105
Anthocyanidins, 89–91
Artemisia acetylenes, 22
Aspartic acid, formation of, 6
  as precursor, 112
Atromentin, 84–85
Aureusidin, 87
Auroglaucin, 29–30
Aurones, 87–90
Azaserine, 124–125

B

Bacitracins, 127–130
Bacteria, carotenoids from, 67
  peptides from 127–131
Barley, alkaloids from 134–135
Belladine (*see* norbelladine)
Benzylisoquinolines (*see* isoquinoline)
Berberine, 111, 116–117
Betanin, 113–114
Bisabolene, 55–56
Biochanin-A, 88
Blowfly larvae, 124
Butein, 87

C

C_1 pool, origin of, 6
  (*see also* S-Adenosylmethionine)
Cadaverine, 110
Cadinene, 56–57

143

Author Index